RUINS
AND
OLD TREES
ASSOCIATED WITH REMARKABLE EVENTS
IN
ENGLISH
HISTORY

LONDON:

HARVEY AND DARTON,

GRACECHURCH STREET.

Also from Westphalia Press

westphaliapress.org

Ruins and Old Trees
Associated with
Memorable Events in English History

by Mary Roberts

WESTPHALIA PRESS
An imprint of Policy Studies Organization

Ruins and Old Trees Associated with Memorable Events in English History
All Rights Reserved © 2016 by Policy Studies Organization

Westphalia Press
An imprint of Policy Studies Organization
1527 New Hampshire Ave., NW
Washington, D.C. 20036
info@ipsonet.org

ISBN-13: 978-1-63391-379-0
ISBN-10: 1-63391-379-1

Cover design by Taillefer Long at Illuminated Stories:
www.illuminatedstories.com

Daniel Gutierrez-Sandoval, Executive Director
PSO and Westphalia Press

Updated material and comments on this edition
can be found at the Westphalia Press website:
www.westphaliapress.org

RUINS AND OLD TREES,

ASSOCIATED WITH

MEMORABLE EVENTS IN ENGLISH HISTORY.

BY

MARY ROBERTS,

AUTHOR OF

"THE PROGRESS OF CREATION, CONSIDERED WITH REFERENCE TO THE
PRESENT CONDITION OF THE EARTH," "CONCHOLOGIST'S COMPANION," &c.

WITH

ILLUSTRATIONS FROM DESIGNS BY GILBERT,
ENGRAVED BY FOLKARD.

THE QUEEN'S OAK

The Oak of Chatsworth,

PLANTED BY HER MAJESTY WHEN PRINCESS VICTORIA.

WAVE on, ye old memorial trees,
In the wintry wind and the summer breeze:
Beacons ye are of days gone by,
Of grief and crime, of the tear and sigh.
Ah! may they never come again,
In hut or hall, on hill or plain!

But a young tree is growing,
Where clear streams are flowing;
Its roots are deep in the mother earth,
In the parent soil that gave it birth,
And its noble boughs are waving high,
Meeting the breeze or the summer wind's sigh;
While quivering lights and shadows play
  On the flowery sod beneath;
And flocks lie down in the heat of day,
  'Mid the fragrant thyme and heath.

a 3

Old trees have fallen down,
   From the sites where they stood of yore,
And now in tower or town
   Their names are heard no more.
When they stood in their days of pride,
   The Saxon wore his crown,
And oft through the forest wide
   The Norman wound his horn;
But thou in thy beauty's sheen,
   Young tree, art rising high,
Thy waving boughs are seen,
   Against the clear blue sky.

No dibbling foot of sportive fawn,
   In silent glen or glade,
No squirrel bounding o'er the lawn
   Thy tender cradle made :
But the poet's eye back glancing,
   Can sing of thy natal day,
When the streamlets in light seem'd dancing,
   And the woods did their homage pay.

A maiden placed thee, forest tree,
   Where thou art standing now,
No care depress'd her thoughts of glee,
   No crown was on her brow ;

But she stood, a lov'd and loving one,
  By her noble mother's side,
And while that gentle deed was done,
  Hearts turn'd to her with pride.

The old memorial trees,
  That rise on rock or glen,
Dark years of human sorrow
  Are chronicled on them ;
But Chatsworth's young oak springing,
  May spread her branches fair,
When nought of sin or sadness
  Shall vex the earth or air.

The crowns which God hath given,
  Shall press not then as now ;
No sceptre shall be riven,
  No care shall cloud the brow.
Victoria ! shielded by His power,
Be thine to triumph in that hour,
Queen of the sea-girt isle ! Not then,
As now, the Queen of suffering men,
But reigning still, beloved and glorious,
O'er sin, and grief, and death victorious.

CONTENTS.

Melksham Court.

Ruins of Bradgate Palace.

Remains of Dunmow Priory.

Gospel-Beech.

Contents. xiii

Clipstone Palace and the Parliament Oak.

Ruined Villages in the New Forest.

Old Trees in Hyde Park.

Contents.

MELKSHAM COURT

Melksham Court.

"I stood in the ruined hall where my ancestors once dwelt. I asked for the noble owners. Where are they?—and the echo replied, Where are they?"

In the midst of the lone forest which shadowed in ancient times a large portion of the country of the Dobuni,* and which extended over hill and dale, far as the distant mountains of the Silures,† and on either side the river that waters this part of Britain, stood a solitary yew. On the verge of the forest, and in places cleared of timber for the purpose, rose the conically-shaped huts of the natives; the dwelling of the chieftain was somewhat larger than the rest, and around it stood the wattled cabins of his dependents. Their arts were few and simple, and their habits those of men who were scarcely advanced beyond a savage state: corn was occasionally cultivated, but in general they lived by hunting,

---

* Gloucestershire. † South Wales.

or fed upon the flocks which they pastured in the open country.

Years passed on, and while the aspect of nature remained the same, all else was changed. This part of Britain bore no longer the appellation of Dobuni; a term derived from the British word Duffen, because the inhabitants frequently resided in places which lay low, and were sunk under hills. It formed a considerable portion of Britannia Superior, and along the side of its beautifully wooded hills, and on its thickly peopled plains, palaces and forums, extensive military roads, aqueducts and schools were rapidly erected. The rattling of heavy-laden cars, and the loud sound of the woodman's axe, with the crash of stately trees, made way for these improvements. In the course of a few short years, the country of the Dobuni lost its wild and forest-like appearance, and far as the eye could reach, the wide-spread landscape presented objects of fertility and beauty. The ancient forest was also curtailed of its grandeur and extent; and the plain country, whose rank luxuriant vegetation concealed marshes, on which it was rarely safe to tread, except in seasons of great drought, was cleared, and thrown open to the sun, and being quickly drained, was covered with towns and villages; corn-fields and meadows succeeded to a growth of underwood, and sheep and oxen grazed where the wolf had been. Sounds too, which of all others awaken images of security and peace—the bleating of sheep along the hills, and the lowing of oxen in the valleys, were heard, instead of the piercing cries of those wild creatures, when ranging in quest of prey. Meanwhile the ample river, whose capricious windings could only be distinguished from the highest hills, was disclosed to view, by the clearing away of tangled bushes, and the cutting down of the huge trees that encroached upon, or shaded its bright waters. The small skin-boats of the natives, and the stately galleys of the Romans, glided along its surface, and commodities of various kinds were brought from one part of the country to the other.

But the day arrived when the galley was rarely seen upon the river. When the skin-boats of the natives ceased to spread abundance along its shores; when many large and fair dwellings were deserted; and when the rolling of chariots, filled with patrician families, whose villas had been erected in some of the most beautiful parts of the country, were no longer heard on the great military road that led from the city of Corinium. Instead of these, bands of armed men spread over the land, for the Roman legions were withdrawn, to save the capital from spoliation, and nothing remained for the unhappy Britons but servitude or death. The Saxons came, for such were the strangers called: their looks were bland, and their flowing vestments, adorned with borders of many colours, betokened some degree of civilization; but war was in their hearts, and soon, where cities had stood, and peaceful homesteads met the view, all was silence and desolation. No curling smoke was seen among the trees, the watch-dog's bark had ceased, there were no flocks for him to guard, and only blackened ruins told of what had been. Gradually, however, a better state of things arose; the Saxons contrasted their past condition, their rude huts on the far off shore, their precarious mode of life, with the elegances, and the per-fection in the arts and sciences which they observed in the homes which they had won. They learned to adopt the habits and the manners of the Romanized Britons, and to repair the desolations which they had wrought. Kingdoms were established, and though war occasionally prevailed among the chieftains, there were many who appreciated the blessings, and the security of peace.

Next came the Danes, men of stern countenances and ruddy hair. War-chiefs, accustomed to a life of rapine—they knew no pity; and what the Saxon would have spared, when first he trod the shores of Britain, they ruthlessly overthrew. The forest and vale country around the solitary yew, was grievously infested with them. They took shelter in the hollows with which this part of England abounded, and it was difficult to dis-possess them. Those hollows or little glens were so deep and narrow, that the rays of the sun frequently did not enliven them for months together; yet still some of the most accessible were brought into cultivation, and rewarded the industrious husbandman with plentiful crops of corn and grass. Others remained in their native wildness, and wild indeed they were. Shallow streams ran through them, and by means of these they could alone be visited: he who sought to explore their secret recesses must force his way beside the channel of the stream; now stepping from stone to stone amid the water's splash; now clinging to the branches of the trees which drooped on either side. But whether wild or cultivated, there the Danes settled themselves, till they were driven out in the days of Alfred.

Alfred established his throne in righteousness, and the country became respectable and happy. Still the tree grew on, and lifted up its head above the boughs of less stately trees, for the yew does not attain to its highest elevation, or rest in the grandeur of its maturity, till five hundred years have passed away, and when the period arrived, concerning which I shall have to speak, the tree was only in its prime.

The forest had encroached upon the precincts of the fields and meadows, during those disastrous times when the ground was trod by hostile steps, as if it sought to recover its ancient rights; but this might not be, and when peace was restored, the sound of the woodman's axe was heard again, and the usurping trees fell beneath its stroke. Then, also, many of those whose ample branches had long sheltered the margin of the cleared land, were cut down, to make room for wider clearings; and by degrees the noble yew, which had been in the depth of the dark forest, stood but a little distance from

the verge of the common, up which the road led, and
which being kept free from trees was reserved for the
pasturing of sheep. It was covered with short grass and
tufts of wild thyme, round which the bees came hum-
ming; and gay flowers, such as the bee-orchis, and the
yellow cistus, the pink-eyed pimpernell, and yellow
rocket, grew profusely beside the pathway. From the
summit of the hill extended a noble panoramic view of
hill and dale. Downward, and far as the eye could
reach, a precipitous descent toward the vale country was
covered with the trees of the old forest, which had gra-
dually been curtailed of its extent; towns and villages
varied the plain, through which the river flowed, and the
strong castles of Dursley and Berkeley, of Beverstone and
Brimpsfield, with their ample hunting-grounds, and the
crowding dwellings of those who lived near, were seen at
intervals.

Generations came and went, and successive monarchs
filled the English throne, till the time of Harold, when
on the battle-field of Hastings his noble patrimony
passed into the hands of the proud Norman. Great
changes then took place; strong castles were erected on
the site of ancient Saxon fortresses, and while seed-time
and harvest did their work, and gradually advanced
and retreated, so gradually did the country emerge from
out the darkness of past ages, and attain an eminence
among the nations of the earth. But as night succeeds
to day, and clouds obscure the cheerful light of the bright

sun, so did war succeed to peace, and ruthless men made sorrowful the homes of England. When Stephen and the empress battled for pre-eminence, fell sounds broke up the quiet of the valleys, and fugitives often sought to hide themselves in the still close covert of the forest.

A gay pageant passed one day within sight of the noble yew. Men carrying branches of the beech, and damsels with flowers in their hands, wound up the road; and with them came a train of oxen, dragging a large tree, which had been cut from out the forest. The tree was wreathed with flowers; the horns of the oxen too were tastefully adorned, and when they reached the summit of the hill, the tree was set up, round which the light-hearted party danced right merrily. All this was done in honour of king Richard's marriage. He had sought the sister of the Emperor Wenceslaus, fair Anne of Luxemburg; and when, at length, the final arrangements were adjusted, she left the palace of her brother, attended by the Duke of Saxony, and a great number of knights and damsels, with men-at-arms, and a goodly company, all well appointed to do her honour. They journeyed through Brabant to Brussels, where the Duke and Duchess received the young queen with great respect, and caused her attendants to be honourably entertained, for the Duke was her uncle, and he rejoiced much in the prospects of his niece. Anne expected merely to have spent a few pleasant days in the society of the Duke and Duchess, but, when about to leave them, intelligence was brought

that twelve large Norman vessels, well equipped, and
filled with armed men, were cruising in the sea between
Calais and Holland, and that, under the pretence of
seizing all who fell into their hands, they were really
waiting for the coming of the lady, whom the king of
France was desirous of getting into his possession, that he
might frustrate the intended alliance between the English
and Germans.   The young queen was exceedingly
alarmed at such unexpected intelligence.   She remained
in consequence with her uncle and aunt, till the
Lords de Roasselaus and de Bousquehoir, having
been deputed by the Duke to negotiate with the King
of France, obtained passports for the safe conveyance of
Anne and her attendants through his dominions, as far
as Calais, as also for the remanding of the Normans into
port.

The young queen then set forwards, after taking leave
of her august relations and the ladies of the court, who
witnessed her departure with much regret.   The Duke
added to her train five hundred spears, and, as she passed
through Ghent and Bruges, the citizens received her with
the utmost honour.   Thus she journeyed on, till being
arrived at Gravelines, the earls of Salisbury and Devon-
shire approached to do her homage, with five hundred
spears, and as many archers.   They conducted her to
Calais, and, having safely confided her to the care of the
English barons, who were appointed to that honour by
the king, they returned homeward.   Great was the joy of

the Londoners, when the train, having passed over the sea to Dover, came within sight of the city gates. Ladies of the highest rank were assembled to receive their queen, all in their best attire, and with them came the great authorities both of the court and city. The gates were then thrown open with much solemnity, and Anne of Luxemburg having been conducted with chivalrous magnificence to the Palace of Westminster, the ceremony of her marriage was completed on the twentieth day after Christmas.

Christmas was well kept that year both in town and country; but when the trees burst forth into leaf and beauty, and the contented note of the solitary cuckoo, was heard in the still forest, the country people thought that they would rejoice again, and this occasioned the May-pole to be set up. They did not gather any branches from the yew, for the yew is a funereal tree, used to deck the grave of him who has nought to do with the cheerful scenes of busy life.

With the noble train who entered London came Margaret of Silesia, daughter of the Duke of Theise, and niece to the King of Bohemia, as the confidential friend, and first-cousin of the queen. This lady was received with great distinction, and apartments were assigned her in the palace, not only on account of her youth, but that she might enjoy a frequent intercourse with the friend who was most dear to her. But these halcyon days were not of long continuance. The queen died at Shene in

Surry, and so bitterly did the king bewail her loss, that he denounced a malediction on the scene of her last illness, and commanded, in the wildness of his grief, that not one stone should be left upon another of the palace where she died. Margaret felt the death of the queen severely; she loved her cousin with a sister's love, and the circumstance of their having left their native land together, and their being to each other what none else could be in a foreign country, had formed between them a bond of no common interest.

The queen deceased without children; but Margaret having married a gentleman of the ducal family of Norfolk, knight of the garter and standard-bearer of England, their only child and heiress, Alana, became the wife of Sir William Tyndale, who was equally respectable in point of antiquity and alliances. His family possessed the valuable domain and title of Tyndale in Northumberland, so called from the south Tyne, which, rising in the mountains and moors of Cumberland, waters that dale, and having joined the north Tyne near Hexham, falls into the German ocean at Tynmouth. Their baronial residence rose proudly on an eminence which commanded the southern banks of the river. It consisted of a spacious antique quadrangle; the roof and walls being of immense strength and thickness, extended in the form of the letter H; the whole was defended by a fosse, and surmounted with four principal towers, in the position of north and south.

> "That castle rose upon the steep, of the green vale of Tyne ;
> While far below, as low they creep,
> From pool to eddy dark and deep,
> Where alders bend and willows weep,
> You hear her streams repine."

The ancestral history of Margaret of Silesia, with that of her distinguished husband, was of no ordinary kind. Her paternal ancestors had filled for ten generations the throne of Poland, and on her mother's side she represented Winceslaus the Good, nearly the last of the ancient kings of Bohemia, as also the imperial houses of Luxemburg and Austria. Among the distinguished crowd of those who figured greatly in by-gone days, Piastus is the one, concerning whom I would briefly speak. His character, seen only through the twilight of remote antiquity, is necessarily involved in great obscurity, but light enough remains to discover the moral grandeur of its proportions, as well as to justify the curiosity of his descendants.

Ancient Polish chronicles relate concerning him, that after the tragical catastrophe of Popiel II., when a dreadful famine added to the calamities of the country, and people fell dead in the streets of Cruswitz, that two angels, in the disguise of pilgrims knocked at the door of a private citizen, named Piastus, and asked for relief. The citizen had only a single cask, which contained some nutritive beverage of the country, remaining in his house, but he would not refuse to help them, and he invited the strangers to partake. Charmed with his benevolence, they promised him the vacant throne, at the same time directing him to open his doors and draw for the relief of the famished population. He did so, and found his cask inexhaustible. The assembled crowds, in their transports, shouted, A miracle! and with one consent elevated their benefactor to the sovereignty of Poland.

From this period the history, both of prince and people, became the subject of authentic narrative. Piastus, like another Numa, retained in his elevation the virtues attributed to him in his private life. The Polish nobles, although accustomed to sanguinary catastrophes, felt their fierceness subside beneath the sway of a monarch who reigned only to make his people happy. He died at an advanced age, beloved, revered, and almost adored by his subjects; and, after the lapse of nearly a thousand years, the name of Piastus is yet repeated with affectionate veneration.

Such is the brief biographical memoranda, which it is possible to rescue from oblivion, concerning the remote ancestry of Margaret of Silesia. She came with great pomp and splendour to the shores of England, and curious has it been to see, while the stream of time flowed on, how some of the noble of the earth, her immediate descendants, were upborn upon its billows; how, in one case, knights and squires represented an elder branch, sober citizens a younger, and how, in a third, the lordly line sunk suddenly beneath the billows.

When the battle of Touton, in the year 1460, made it

unsafe for those who adhered to the house of Lancaster to remain in public, the immediate descendant of Margaret, in that branch which is associated with the aged yew, withdrew from his paternal estate and settled in Glouces-tershire, where he assumed the name of Hitchen. He married Alicia, daughter and sole heiress of Hunt of Hunt's Court, in Nibley, by whom he acquired that estate, and became the grandfather of William Tyndale, who is justly termed the apostle of the English Reformation.

As the gathering mists of a hot summer evening, when the sun is set, and dew begins to fall, veil the bold and prominent landscape, so the obscurity of time has settled on the Tyndale family. The outlines yet remain: the establishment of Hugh Tyndale in Gloucestershire, during the troubles of York and Lancaster, his marriage with Alicia, and the birth of his three grandsons, John, William, and Thomas, are events well known; but whether Tyndale suffered a long imprisonment in the castle of Vilvorde, near Louvain in Flanders, during the lifetime of his parents; whether days of sorrow and nights of weariness befell them on his account; or whether they were first laid to rest in Nibley churchyard, near which their mansion stood, is entirely unknown. Be this as it may, his brother Thomas had much to suffer on his account. He was abjured for receiving letters, and for remitting him five marks during his residence in Flanders.

Time went on, and religious animosities gradually subsided; a descendant of Hugh Tyndale purchased

Melksham Court in Stinchcombe, on the verge of all that remained of the once great forest. It was a beautiful spot, embosomed in trees, and moated according to the olden fashion, with its terrace-walks and parterres. There his descendants continued to reside, and their days seem to have passed tranquilly, till the stormy reign of Charles I.

The valleys of Gloucestershire lying remote from the metropolis, and being in many respects almost inaccessible, from the steepness of the hills, having also no great public road near at hand, nor the sea within reach, had been often spared from much suffering in very disastrous times; it was otherwise at the present day. The forest, one of their great bulwarks, had been curtailed during successive generations, and much of the moor country having been brought into cultivation, towns and villages were built, and roads were made from place to place. This opened a communication with the thickly peopled parts of Gloucestershire, with such counties also as lay contiguous : the quiet of the valleys was therefore broken up, and the cities of Gloucester and of Worcester, having taken active parts in the stirring incidents of the time, bands of armed men overspread the country. Thomas Tyndale, the fifth in descent from the purchaser of Melksham Court, was then residing on his patrimonial estate : he married a lady on her mother's side, of the knightly family of Poyntz of Iron Acton; but whether—for the mists of time have settled again on the domestic incidents of the family—whether his lady was deceased, or whether he had sent her with their young son and four daughters to a place of greater security, cannot be ascertained. Certain it is, that seeing a band of armed men advancing to the house, he fled for shelter into the forest which skirted his domain. The forest could afford but little aid in his distress. It was otherwise when its crowding trees extended further than the eye could reach, now sinking into the deep, deep glens, whose circling banks, if such they might be termed, rose far above its topmost boughs; now ascending those high banks, and spreading over the vale country, sinking and rising with the undulations of hill and dale, and, when the wind howled among the branches, appearing like the tossing waves of a restless sea. This had been; but cultivation trenched upon the good green wood; spaces were even cleared, and its tall trees, for all the underwood was gone, afforded a ready access to whoever liked to invade its beautiful recesses. One hope for safety remained to the fugitive, and one only. The yew-tree stood in all its beauty and luxuriance, near to the summit of Stinchcombe wood, for such the old forest was now called, and thither he fled for shelter. He was seen to leave the house by a band of soldiers, and they hastened in pursuit of him. They thought that he would make for the nearest glen, or else that he would seek to hide himself in some sheltered nook among the trees. Heaven, in its mercy, prevented them from searching the old tree, whose intermingling branches formed a close and impervious shelter. Yet they passed, and repassed, beneath the shade, and their words were hard to bear. They vowed to have no pity on him, nor on his children, nor on anything that he possessed; and they said, " that if they could discover him in his retreat, they would hew him small as herbs for a porridge-pot." Being foiled in their search, they wreaked their vengeance on his mansion, and during his dolorous sojourn of three days and nights in the tree, he saw the burning of his once happy home, and heard at intervals the voices of his pursuers, as they sought for him again, among the glens, and through the secret passes of the wood. We know not how, nor when the family were reunited ; nor can I speak concerning the joys and thankfulness with which they met, for the mists of time rest on this also.

The yew-tree is still standing; around it are the remains of the old forest, and beside it the wild common, with its thyme and flowers among the grass. All else has changed since the days when the noble ancestor of him who fled for refuge to the ample branches of the yew, first landed on the English coast. Neither is the surrounding country such as it was, in the days of Richard. The castles of Beverstone, of Brimsfield, and Dursley, whose turrets were seen in ancient times from the summits of the hill, are fallen to decay, and instead of these, modern dwellings, with parks and gardens, farms and cottages, overspread the country. The cheerful farm-house, with its lofty rookery, and wide arable, or ploughed fields, with low fences or gray stone walls, are prominent features in the southern portion of the landscape; as also well-timbered villages, occasional heaths, and tufted woods, or rather groves. At the end of summer, the strong colours of the yellow wheat and glaring poppy are finely contrasted with the dark hue of the woods; that hue which becomes deeper and more sombre, till the night-dews have done their work, and the autumnal winds begin to blow, and the dark green leaves are suddenly invested with a splendid variety of tints, from bright yellow to the deepest orpiment.

On the verge of the old forest extend rural villages and fertile meadows, high-aspiring elms, shallow brooks, and wooden bridges, crowding cottages and green lanes, with here and there a church-spire, or gray tower rising among the trees. Gentle swells and hollows, where sheep pasture on the green sward, are seen in another portion of the landscape, with apple-orchards and small enclosures; but along the banks of the Severn the country assumes a different aspect. Its general characteristics are breaks of lawn and thicket, with groves and stunted pollards, all footed and entangled with briars and creeping plants.

A dilapidated court-house, overrun with ivy, and

near it an aged church, may be seen by him who knows their locality, from the summit of Stinchcombe hill. The church is the waymark, for the walls of the old court are low, and it is only when the wind favours the sight of them, by causing the branches of near trees to bend beneath its sway, that even the church-tower can be discerned among the young green foliage of the spring. The gardens of the once stately mansion are gone to decay, or else, being overgrown with grass, are fed upon by cattle; the windows were broken by the fierceness of the flames when it was set on fire; and though strong walls, still standing, tell of what has been, not a trace remains of the great oriel window, and the roof has long been gone. He who wishes to trace the former extent of the building may just discover the foundations in some parts; but in others, not even a few scattered stones, sunk deep in the untrodden grass, would reveal that a mansion had stood there.

Yet Nibley Court once occupied that spot; there a happy family dwelt, and busy scenes went on—the sports of childhood, and the daily incidents of domestic life. There my ancestors resided. But all are gone, and scarcely-discovered ruins, which, as regard all grandeur of appearance, might have belonged to a barn or an out-house, alone remain.

The yew-tree still lives, but that also betokens the lapse of time. Its once ample boughs are few; they

yield no shelter now; the blue sky may be seen through
them; the stem also teaches that ages have passed away,
since it bore up a noble canopy of mingled boughs.   A
rabbit from the warren on the common might run up
the scarred trunk, but it could not find a hiding-place
among the scattered branches.

BRADGATE PALACE

Bradgate Palace.

"This was thy home then, gentle Jane,
   This thy green solitude ;—and here
At evening, from thy gleaming pane,
   Thine eye oft watch'd the dappled deer,
While the soft sun was in its wane,
   Browsing beneath the brooklet clear ;
The brook runs still, the sun sets now,
   The trees wave still ; but where art thou ?"

A rocky bank, with scattered sheep, are objects on which the mind loves to rest. Such is the back-ground of Bradgate ruin, the birth-place of the beautiful Jane Grey, the illustrious and ill-fated scion of the house of Suffolk, concerning whom it was related by one who had seen and loved her, that even in her eighteenth year she had the innocence of childhood, the beauty of youth, the solidity of middle, and the gravity of old age ; the life of a saint, and yet the death of a malefactor. On that rocky bank she had often gazed, for though man passes from his inheritance, and noble dwellings crumble to the dust, nature changes not. Rude eminences extend further back, on which the wild rose and sweet-briar have long fixed themselves, with bramble-bushes, ferns, and fox-glove; they are skirted by low and romantic dingles, where sheep pasture, and butterflies sport from one flower to another. He who approaches the old ruin, from the little village of Cropston, can hardly picture to himself that time has done its work in laying low the ancient palace of the Greys. On the left, stands that noble group of chesnut-trees, under the shade of which little Jane used to play; on the right extends a slate coppice, intermingled with moss and flowers, in beautiful contrast with the deep shade of the old chesnuts, the roots of which are laved by the clear trout-stream, on which stood a corn-mill in Leland's days;—" that faire and plentiful springe of water, brought by master Brok, as a man would judge, agayne the hille, thorough the lodge, and thereby it dryveth the mylee." The mill came into decay when the mansion was deserted, and no one went thither for the grinding of his corn; some of the large stones fell into the stream, and interrupted for a short space the rapid flowing of the water, and among them grow the water-dock and bulrush, with large river-weeds and trailing plants. Again it hurries on, dancing from amid the roots and broken masses of huge stones, clear and sparkling, and fringed with ferns and flowers, the delight of Jane, when she used to watch beside it with Elmer, that " deare friend and schoolmaster, who taught her so gently and yet so pleasantly, that she

thought the time as nothing, while she was with him."
This streamlet laves in its course the once hospitable
mansion of the Greys, and passes from thence into the
fertile meadows of Smithland. Beautiful too is the vale
of Newtown, lonely yet romantic, the favourite resort of
all who delight in the sylvan solitudes of nature—where,
as legends tell, Jane used to walk—with its hill and tower
in the distance, the nearest neighbours of Bradgate Palace,
now, like that, all roofless and deserted. What a contrast,
in its loneliness, to the busy tide of care, ever rolling on, in
the ancestral halls, the towns and villages, that vary the
mighty landscape, which extends before the elevated
solitude, with its aged ruin! That ruin was dwelt in
once, not by the owl and bat, its sole tenants now, but
by living men and women, who held pleasant intercourse
with the inhabitants of Bradgate Palace; with dwellers
too, in places, the sites of which, grass has long grown
over, or which the antiquary can hardly trace. Woods
and fields and streamlets are seen from the same high
hill; wide commons and quiet valleys, with dells and
dingles; and above them extends the glorious dome of
heaven, where light summer-clouds are speeding, and
the bright sun looks down on the lovely scene beneath.

Back to my old ruin—for high hills, and far off scenes,
are not the objects of my search. Back to my old ruin,
which stands alone in its desolation, while all around is
verdurous and joyful. Full shining on it, are the warm
beams of a summer sun, and soft breezes shake the tufts

of ferns and wallflowers that spring from out the crannies, the rents of ruin, which time has made in the old walls. Butterflies shut and open their gorgeous wings on the golden disk of that bright flower, which loves to fling its friendly mantle over fallen greatness, and now carpets with luxuriant vegetation the broken pavement, through the interstices of which its broad leaves rise up. Birds are singing on the trees, and bees come humming to gather pollen from the flowers of the noble chesnuts that droop in all their beauty and luxuriance over the old ruins. Those who have long ceased from among the living used to gaze on them, and gather their beautiful tufts of pyramidical white flowers with which to adorn the open spaces in the oriel window. They grew here far back as the reign of Edward, when the great park of Bradgate, with its circumference of seven miles, came into the possession of the Earl of Ferrars, for the chesnut is a tree of long duration, and the stately group is beginning to decline. Little now remains of the once princely mansion, the palace, large and fair and beautiful, as wrote the historian Fuller. The walls are low and roofless, broken and dismantled, and scarcely is it possible to point out the different apartments that once resounded with cheerful voices. All is still and lonely now; the tilt-yard is nearly perfect, but none are playing there; the garden-walls, with their broad terrace-walks, remain entire, but none are walking there; gray and yellow lichens, with tufts of moss, dot over the old stones, and so wild and high has grown the grass, that it looks as if no one had trodden there for ages. A noble pleasure-ground formerly extended round the mansion, and beyond it was the spacious park, where the duke and duchess, the parents of Lady Jane, with all the house-hold, gentlemen and gentlewomen, used to hunt. Traces of walks and alleys, and broad spaces for exercise or pleasure are still visible, though generations have passed away since the members of the house of Groby sauntered among them, and the place has much the appearance of a wilderness; yet the aspect is not that of total wildness, of a spot where the hand of man has never been; indi-cations everywhere present themselves, that where the nettle, and the dandelion, with its golden petals and sphere of down, reign undisturbed, the rose and lily once grew luxuriantly. The house too, how desolate and changed! The earls of Leicester, of Hinton, and of Ferrars presided here; then came Sir Edward Grey, Lord Ferrars of Groby, and then the Earl of Hunting-don. Here also resided the Marquis of Dorset, the son-in-law of him who wedded the Dowager Queen of France, Charles Brandon, "cloths of gold and freize," as sung the courtly poet, when contrasting his own con-dition with that of the widowed queen.

> " Cloth of freize, be not too bold,
>   Though thou art matched with cloth of gold;
>   Cloth of gold, do not despise,
>   Though thou art matched with cloth of frieze."

C

Tradition points through the dim vista of long ages to a broken tower, as the one where Lady Jane resided, and which bears her name. Beside it is a chapel, wherein are effigies of Lord Grey of Groby, and the Lady Grey, his wife. The chapel is carefully preserved, but all else are in ruins :—the tower, the great hall, the state apartment, the refectory, the tennis-court, nothing remains of them but lichen-tinted walls, or ruins black with smoke. Here then, amid lone ruins and green trees, beside the streamlet's rush and the old grove of chesnuts, where the lavrock and the titlark, the gold-finch and the thrush are singing, with no companions but rejoicing birds and flowers, let me recall the mournful realities of bygone days.

" Here, in departed days, the gentle maid,
    The lovely and the good, with infant glee,
  Along the margin of the streamlet play'd,
    Or gathered wild flowers 'neath each mossy tree ;
  And little recked what cares were her's to be,
    While listening to the skylark's soaring lay,
  Or merry grasshopper that carolled free,
    In verdant haunts, throughout the livelong day,
    That beauteous child, as blithe, as sorrowless as they.

" And here, where sighs the summer breeze among
    These echoing halls, deserted now and bare,
  Oft o'er some tome of ancient lore she hung,—
    No student ever since so wondrous fair !
  Or lifted up her soul to God in prayer,
    And pondered on his verse, of price untold,
  Radiant with wisdom's gems beyond compare,
    Richer than richest mines of purest gold,—
    The star that guides our steps safe to the Saviour's fold.

" To fancy's wizard gaze, fleet o'er yon height,
 Hunters and hounds tumultuous sweep along;
And many a lovely dame and youthful knight
 Gaily commingle with the stalwarth throng
Of valiant nobles, famed in olden song;
 But not amid them, as they rapid ride,
Is that meek damsel—trained by grievous wrong
 Of haughty parents to abase her pride,
 Ere yet her lot it was to be more sternly tried.

" Here from her casement, as she cast a look,
 Oft might she mourn their reckless sport to scan;
And well rejoice to find, in classic book,
 Solace,—withdrawn from all that pleasure can
Impart to rude and riot-loving man:
 Aye, and when at the banquet, revels ran
To loud extreme, she here was wont to haste,
 And marvel at Creation's mighty plan;
Or with old bards and sages pleasure taste,
Unknown to Folly's crowd, whose days all run to waste

" And thus it was—the child of solitude,
 She grew apart, beneath that Father's eye
Who careth for the wild-birds' nestling brood,
 And decks the flow'ret with its varied dye;
 Nor, in His presence, had she cause to sigh
For the vain pageants of delusive mirth;
 Trained to uplift her soul, in musing high,
From this dark vale of wretchedness and dearth,
Aloft, above the stars, where angels have their birth.

" Well had she need! a scaffold was the path
 To that abode her soul had often sought;
Scarce crowned before the stormiest clouds of wrath
 Rolled o'er her head, with scathing ruin fraught.
 Alas, for human greatness! it is nought!
And nought she found it, save a deadly snare,
 Enchantment, by the evil genii wrought,
Whose diadems conceal the brow of care;
Whose tissued robes display a lustre false, as fair.

" Beautiful martyr! widowed by the hand
    That reft thee of thy life, ere yet 'twas thine ;
Thy grave to find beneath a guilty land,
    Thou hast no need of gilded niche or shrine !
    Fond recollections round thy memory twine—
A sacred halo circles thy brief years ;
    'Tis thine, redeemed from sin and death, to shine
Eternally above this world of fears:
Where Christ himself, thy King, hath wiped away all tears.

" Farewell, thou mouldering relic of the past !
    An hour unmeetly was not spent with thee :
Events as rapid as the autumn's blast
    Have hurried onward, since 'twas thine to see
    The fairest flower of England pensively
Expand and blossom 'neath thy rugged shade ;
    And here thou stand'st, while circling seasons flee,
A monumental pile of that sweet maid,
Whom men of cruel hands within the charnel laid."

              The Author of the Visions of Solitude.

GLENDOUR'S OAK

Glendour's Oak.

> " Survivor sole, and hardly such, of all
>   That once lived here, thy brethren:
>   A shatter'd veteran, hollow trunk'd,
>   And with excoriate forks deformed—
>   Relic of ages."

SUCH is the Oak of Chertsey, that celebrated tree, over which the storms of many centuries have passed. The sunny bank on which it grows is covered with primroses and cowslips, and among them the little pimpernel and violet lift up their modest heads. Tufts of eyebright, with cuckoo-flowers and sweet woodroof, grow also, beside the hollies and stunted hawthorns, which are seen upon the common; their fragrant flowers and green leaves present a striking contrast to the time-worn tree; the one tells of other days, of ages that have passed since its stately stem arose in all the grandeur of sylvan majesty; the other, in their freshness and their loveliness, breathe only of youth and beauty.

The view is somewhat confined, but the eye that likes to rest on a quiet home-scene finds much in it to admire.

An ample river winds through green meadows, with trees on either side, and, in the distance, is a church with its solitary turret, and rude porch of the olden time. The gentle murmur of a stream is heard at intervals, and the sighing of the wind among the branches of the aged oak; on high the lark lifts up his song of joy, and the warbling of birds breaks upon the stillness of the place; that of the chaffinch and the throstle, the goldfinch and the linnet, and the sweet full tone of the contented blackbird. They much affect this spot, it is so lone, yet cheerful.

Time was when the site of the old tree resounded with the clang of arms, and rueful sights were seen from its topmost boughs, for the Oak of Chertsey was then in its prime; the now rough and quarried bark was smooth and glossy, and its ample branches sheltered an extensive space, where sheep could lie down at noon.

A dreadful battle was fought between Henry IV. and Hotspur a short way off, and scarcely had any battle occurred in those ages of which the shock was more terrible. Furious and repeated vollies of "arrowy sleet," discharged from the strong bows of Hotspur's archers, did great execution in the royal army; they were showered from a rising ground covered with green sward, on which the shepherds loved to pasture their flocks, and where the village children used to gather cowslips and yellow-cups. But the flocks had been driven off, and the frightened children were in their homes; the rising ground was no place for them. The arrows that were thus furiously

discharged did their work, and many fell; the king's bow-
men were not wanting in return, and the battle raged
with great fury. Henry was in the thickest of the fight,
and his gallant son, who afterwards carried misery and
desolation throughout the fields of France, signalized
himself that day. Percy, too, supported the fame which
he had earned in many a hard-fought battle, and
Douglas, his ancient enemy, though now his friend, still
appeared his rival, amid the horror and confusion of the
scene. He raged through the field in search of the king,
and as Henry, either to elude the vigilance of the enemy,
or to encourage his own men by the belief of his presence
everywhere, had accoutred several captains in the royal
garb, the sword of Douglas rendered this honour fatal
to many. At length the standard of the king, fluttering
high in air, recalled Douglas to the spot, and little heed-
ing the flight of arrows, which rattled on his armour like
hail, nor yet the chosen band who were appointed to
guard the banner, he and his associate Hotspur pierced
their way thither. Henry was thrice unhorsed, and would
have been either taken or slain, had not his men kept
back, with desperate valour, the furious onset of the
assailants, while the Earl of March forced him from the
scene of danger. Yet still they sought him, and having
beaten down his banner, and slain its bearer, with many
of the faithful band appointed to guard the royal flag, vic-
tory began to swerve in favour of the rebel army. But in one
moment a loud voice sounded far and wide over the dread-

ful scene.   It proclaimed, "Hotspur is dead," and with
this thrilling cry ended the conflict of the day.   Douglas,
was taken prisoner, and there fell, on either side,
near two thousand three hundred gentlemen, beside six
thousand private men.

Owen Glendour heard the shout which proclaimed that
his friend had fallen, for he witnessed the battle from the
top of the lofty oak.   He had marched with a large
army to within a mile of Shrewsbury, and if the king had
not proceeded thither with great haste, he would have
joined his friend Hotspur.   A broad and rapid river lay
in front, and he pressed on to cross, if possible, before
the beaming helmets, which he saw advancing rapidly
over the plain country, could reach the town.   But a
heavy rain had fallen, and the water was exceedingly
high; the ford at Shelton was, in consequence, impassable,
and the bridge at Shrewsbury was strongly guarded.
Owen Glendour therefore halted.   He saw with grief
the forces of Hotspur drawn up in order of battle imme-
diately before him, for he knew that he could lend no
assistance, and, when the next morning dawned, the
armies had joined fight.

Owen Glendour then climbed the large oak; of which
the topmost branches afforded a full view of the battle-field
and the surrounding country.   He saw from thence the
furious onset, and heard the shock of battle ; horses and
men contending, and the dreadful shouts which, rever-
berating from the hollows of the hills, sounded like dis-

tant thunder; he heard, too, the one loud voice which told that his friend had fallen.

Owen Glendour returned to his castle in the Vale of Glyndwrdwey: it was situated amid the wildest and the sternest scenery, beside the torrent's roar, and surrounded with all the magnificence of rock and fell. There did he soon assemble to his standard those ardent spirits who preferred death to slavery, and who vowed that the blue hills and the pleasant valleys of their fathers' land should never be subjected to the yoke of a usurper. Daring adventures, and strange escapes by flood and field, marked his onward course. The English regarded him with superstitious dread; the Welch looked to him as one possessed of more than mortal power; and thus during fifteen years did he resist the aggressions of a monarch, whose prowess had long been known, the efforts too of a chivalrous nobility, and a martial people.

Yet Glendour was not designed by nature for a life of daring hardihood and of murderous intent. He was amiable and beloved in private life, and, his parents having designed him for the bar, he was qualifying himself as an able lawyer, when intelligence was brought that Henry IV. had granted a large portion of his paternal acres to Lord Grey of Rhuthin, that treacherous nobleman who had long sought to prejudice the king against him. Owen Glendour closed the book that lay before him; he declared that a descendant of the Princes of Powys was not to be so treated; and having drawn his

sword from out the scabbard, he sheathed it not again
while life remained. A fierce battle, on the banks of the
Evyrnwy, made Lord Grey his prisoner, and the pay-
ment of a thousand marks, with the marriage of his
daughter to that nobleman, alone obtained for him his
liberty.

It was noted that disasters of various kinds attended
the expeditions of King Henry into Wales. The natives
of the country attributed them to the magic powers of
Owen Glendour, whom they believed able to control the
elements, and who, when his men grew faint and weary,
and he himself wished for a short respite from the toils of
war, could pour upon the bands of Henry the fury of the
northern storm. It was said that he could loose the
secret springs of the wild cataract, and cause it to send
forth such a flood of water, that the moors and valleys,
through which the invader had to pass, would seem like
an inland sea. Some believed that he could even summon
the loud thunders from their secret cell, and cause the
forked lightning to strike terror into the stoutest heart;
that in one moment he could not only bring to his
assistance a wild storm from off the hills, but that, when
the beautiful glens and woods appeared in all their loveli-
ness and repose, and every hill was lighted up with a
glorious sunbeam, he could suddenly obscure them with
the darkest shades of night. Thus men thought; they
saw not, in the strange and terrible calamities which con-
tinually opposed the progress of King Henry, a continua-

tion of events which had attended him since the death of
Richard. Richard had been the friend and benefactor of
Glendour; he had fought for him while living, and now that
he was gone, he sought not only to revenge his death, but
to preserve his native land from the usurpations of a
foreign yoke. He performed, in consequence, such feats
of valour, bore up beneath the pressure of such heavy
trials, and devised such masterly schemes to circumvent
the devices of the enemy, as his countrymen believed
could neither be planned nor achieved by mortal mind
or arm. They knew not the strength and the enthusiasm
which injury and oppression will produce in either.
Excited, therefore, to the highest pitch of feeling, Owen
inspired his men with much of his own energy: aided by
them, he foiled the power of the wary and martial Henry,
and drove him ignominiously from the field. At the
head of his choicest armies, the English king had often
to retreat before a handful of men, whose chief had been
unused to a military life; and though Glendour and his
adherents were reduced at times to take shelter in caves
and fastnesses, known only to themselves, they emerged
again, and fell with terrible fury on the English, in
moments, too, when they thought themselves most secure
from their aggressions.

Had Glendour lived in peaceful times, he would have
been a poet of no ordinary rank. The bard Rhys Coch,
was his cotemporary and chosen associate in his
days of woes and wanderings. A stone still remains

near Bethgellert, where the bard used to sit and pour forth the melody of his harp to his own inspiring lays. There, tradition says, Glendour would sit beside him in that beloved retreat, where around them was all the stern majesty of nature, in her darkest, her loneliest, her loveliest moods. The rapid Gwinan prattled near them over her rocky bed, laving on one side green meadows, filled with cowslips and cuckoo-flowers, where cattle feed, and skirted with groves of oak, and ash, and birch; on the other, its bright waters race beside a wild and heathy tract of moorland, which slopes upward to the very base of Snowdon, that king of mountains, whose awful brow is often hidden in the clouds.

The bard, too, had suffered much, and had fled from cave to cave, and from hill to hill, pursued by the English forces, who sought to still those bold and pathetic strains—those deep laments, which aroused his country-men to fresh deeds of valour against their oppressors. His enemies were not permitted to accomplish their designs. He continually eluded their pursuit, and died at length in peace, amid his beloved haunts of Beth-gellert.

Here then stands the ancient tree, though reft of its former greatness. More than four hundred years have elapsed since Owen Glendour climbed its lofty trunk, and surveyed the battle-field of Tewksbury; since his bannered hosts were stationed round, and he heard the shout which told him that his friend had fallen.

From this tree, also, might be heard, in ancient times, the sound of the workman's hammer, for King Henry appointed that a chapel should be built, and two priests placed within it, to pray both morning and evening for the souls of those who had been slain. Rapidly the chapel rose, for men thought that they did good service to their Maker when they wrought in such holy work; and the chapel, being enlarged in after years, became a handsome parish church. The condition of the time-worn tree, and of the church are somewhat similar. The tree is grown so hollow that it seems to stand on little more than a circle of bark, yet life still lingers, green leaves appear in the spring season, and acorns are gathered from its branches in the autumn. Great part of the once stately building has likewise fallen to decay; ivy grows luxuriantly over the broken walls, and sparrows build their nests among the matted branches; but Divine worship is to this day still carried on in the part that remains entire. The country people and neighbouring gentry meet there; they bear the name of Englishmen, though blending in themselves varied and dissimilar races—the ancient Briton and the Roman, the Dane, the Saxon, and the Norman. But how widely different in their habits and their manners from those who assisted in building the ancient chapel, and those who assembled within its walls when the chapel was completed!

Yew-Trees of Skelldale.

The Yew-Trees of Skelldale.

"Worthy indeed of note
Are those fraternal yews of lone Skelldale,
Joined in one solemn and capacious grove;
Huge trunks! and each particular trunk a growth
Of intertwisted fibres serpentine,
Nor uninformed with phantasy, and looks
That threaten the profane; a pillared shade,
Upon whose grassless floor of red-brown hue,
By sheddings from the pining umbrage tinged
Perennially, beneath whose sable roof
Of boughs, as if for festal purpose decked
With unrejoicing berries, ghostly shapes
May meet at noon-tide: Fear and trembling hope,
Silence and foresight—death the skeleton,
And time the shadow—there to celebrate,
As in a natural temple, scatter'd o'er
With altars undisturb'd of mossy stone,
United worship; or in mute repose
To lie and listen to the mountain stream."

WORDSWORTH.

THE busy hum of men has long ceased from the spot
where stand the fraternal yew-trees. Ages have passed
away since the illuminator sat intent on his pleasant
labours in the ruin hard by—since he put aside his liquid

gold and Tyrian purple, and laid him down to rest in the burying-place beside the abbey. The copier of manuscripts closed his book there, more than five hundred years ago ; he, too, is gone, and with him all those who lived while he was living. The abbot, who presided in regal state ; the brotherhood, in their cowls and gowns ; learned men, who studied in their quiet cells, and the busy comers and goers, who worked either in the abbey-fields, or performed such menial labours as the condition of the place required—not a trace of them remains : even the stately monastery is in ruins, but the yew-trees still cast the shadow of their noble branches on the grassless floor of red-brown hue. Their history is inseparably connected with that of the ruined abbey, for they stood in their present site, and afforded a shelter to its founders, long before one stone was laid upon another of the stately building. Those who passed in the days of the Saxon king, Ethelbald, through the Wolds of Yorkshire, near Skelldale, in their way to Ripon, might see a company of men assembled in a wild and romantic spot, watered by a rivulet, and surrounded with rocks and woods. These men were monks, who, desiring to imitate the extraordinary sanctity of the Cistercian abbey of Rieval, had withdrawn from their own monastery of St Mary's at York, and being sanctioned in their preference by the archbishop, they retired to this desolate and uncultivated spot. They had no house to shelter them, nor certainty of provisions to subsist on ; but, in the depth of the lone

valley, stood an aged elm, among the ample branches of
which they erected a straw roof, and this was their only
shelter for some time.   But at length the rain fell fast,
and the wind rose high, and they were constrained to
quit the shelter of the elm for that of seven stately yew-
trees, which grew on the south side of the valley, where
a splendid abbey afterwards arose.   These trees were of
extraordinary size, for the trunk of one of them measured
twenty-six feet in circumference, at the height of three
feet above the root.   Neither history nor tradition have
preserved the knowledge of that period when they first
arose from out the ground.   Ages may have passed
since, and countries rose and waned.   The yew-trees of
Skelldale may have continued growing even from the
brilliant periods of Thebes and Memphis, when Phœnician
barks traded to the Isle of Tin, and all around them was
one wild impenetrable forest.   But the yew-trees were
now in their prime, and beneath them the monks took
shelter by night and by day, from the rain and snow,
and the cold east wind, that swept moaning through the
valley.   Thus they lived, drinking at the stream when
thirsty, and allaying their hunger with the bread which
their archbishop sent them from time to time.   When
the snow melted from the branches of the sheltering
trees, and the cold east wind was still—when the delicate
yellow blossoms of the yew varied its dark funereal
branches, and bees came humming to gather in the
pollen, they cleared a small spot of ground to serve them

as a garden, and built a wooden chapel. Thus they passed the first winter, and their piety was noised abroad. Many repaired to them from distant parts, some for instruction, others to join the fraternity ; and as their numbers increased, their privations increased also. They were often reduced to the necessity of eating the leaves of trees and wild herbs ; but their fortitude did not fail them, and one day when their stock of provisions consisted of merely two loaves and a half, a passing stranger asked for a morsel of bread. " Give him a loaf," said the abbot; " the Lord will provide." The hope thus piously expressed, was soon fulfilled, and a cart piled with bread was seen coming down the rocky pathway, a present from Eustace Fitz-John, owner of the neighbouring castle of Knaresborough.

Time passed on, and none who witnessed the privations which the monks of Skelldale endured, could have pictured to themselves the future greatness of their monastery. Meanwhile, the garden flourished, and fields were added to those which they began to cultivate, till at length, wrote one of the secluses, " We have bread and cheese, butter and ale, and in time we shall have beef and mutton." He lamented that the soil was too poor for the growth of vines ; but he added, " that the garden was well supplied with pot-herbs." Of these he gave no particular description, but we may presume that they consisted of colewort and onions, of peas and beans, of spinach, and radishes with a vegetable called feret, most probably carrot, or

perhaps beet, and a variety of sweet-herbs, for such were
in use among the Saxons.   At length the privations of
the monks of Skelldale ceased, as also the necessity for
labour.   Hugh, Dean of York, bequeathed to them his
wealth, and benefactions having poured in successively,
from different quarters, the abbey became exceedingly
rich in land and cattle, with plate and costly vestments.
A wild and beautiful spot was also bestowed on Fountains
Abbey by the Percy family; this was Walham Cove,
situated among the hilly and mountainous tracts of the
West-Riding of Yorkshire.   It was included in lands
belonging to the manor of Walham, and possessed a
valuable right of fishing in the ample stream that flowed
from out an immense and perpendicular crag of lime-
stone, more than three hundred feet in height, that
stretched across the valley like a magnificent screen.
Thither the monks of Fountains Abbey used to repair;
thither, too, many of those recluses, who wearied with
fights and forage in foreign lands, sought for rest within
the abbey walls, loved to muse and moralize upon the
passing waters.   But they learned not wisdom from them,
nor read in things inanimate, lessons that might have
taught them to retain the habits of their predecessors.
Most of those devoted men, who had sought to worship
their Creator in privacy and stillness, were laid down to
rest.   They had laboured with their hands while living,
and thankfully saw the blessings which they sought,
spring from out the earth they cultivated; those who

filled their places were not actuated by the same
necessity, and hence the passer-by no longer beheld a
humble cloister, with its garden and low fence, but
instead of this a stately building, the Abbey of the
Fountain, as it was called in reference to the stream that
flowed beside it, fresh and untroubled as when the
monks of St. Mary's first sought the precincts of the
dale.   There were many in after years who desired that
their mortal remains might be deposited beneath the abbey
walls, and for this purpose they devised large sums of
money :—some who had been in the deathful career of
storm and siege, and those, the flowers of chivalry, who
had won the prize at tilts and tournaments ; when armed
knight met knight, and high-born ladies gazed on and
awarded the victor's meed.   Rest they had not found on
earth, amid the stunning tide of crime and human care, and
they wished that bells might toll for them, and prayers
be said for them, beside the rushing waters of the Skill.
The mental eye, back glancing, through the vista of long
ages, sees at intervals successive funerals slowly pro-
ceeding through the abbey gates.   Warriors of the noble
house of Percy borne there.   Lord Rieland, one of the
twenty guardians of the Magna Charta, he who sustained
the shock of arms and cheered on his vassals in the
Barons' wars.   He too, Lord Henry de Percy, another
member of that ancient race, who followed in after years
the banner of King Edward into Scotland, was borne by
his tall yeomen to that still and narrow bed which

receives alike the prince and peasant. Others also
followed, great in their day, and filled while living with
busy schemes, but of whom, as years were added, scarcely
a trace remained.—Where knees bent in prayer, and the
white-robed priest chanted the high requiem, a broken
stone figure, recumbent on a lichen-dotted stone, points
out a warrior's resting-place; and perchance a mound
thrown up, with broken slabs of richly-sculptured marble,
indicate that some one who had figured greatly in past
ages lay there; again, a broken crosier, or a pilgrim's
staff, tell of years spent in wanderings, and in prayer.

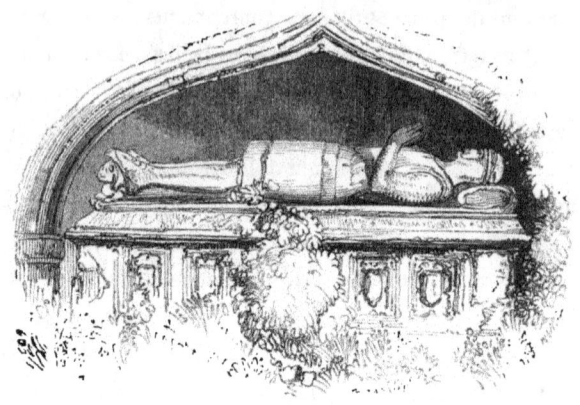

HOWE SELE'S OAK.

Howel Sele's Oak.

"I mark'd a broad and blasted oak,
    Scorched by the lightning's livid glare,
Hollow its stem from branch to branch,
    And all its shrivell'd arms were bare.
E'en to this day, the peasant still,
    With cautious fear, avoids the ground;
In each wild branch a spectre sees,
    And trembles at each rising sound."

How beautiful is this wild spot, with its accompaniments of lawn and thicket, with its clear stream, now prattling over a rocky bed, and now dancing in playful eddies beside the tufts of grass and yellow flowers, that skirt the margin of the water! Innumerable boughs shut out the distant prospect, and neither a church-spire, nor curling smoke, ascending from some lone cottage, betoken the abode of men. In the midst of this fair spot stands a "caverned, huge, and thunder-blasted oak;" its dry branches are white with age, the bark has long since fallen from them, and most impressive is the contrast which it presents to the lightness and the freshness of the young green trees among which it stands, as

among them, though not of them. Beyond their ver-
durous circle are a variety of romantic dingles, covered
with blackberry-bushes, with moss, and ivy. Gigantic
trees fling the shadow of their noble branches over the
green sward, and the spaces between them are filled, here,
and there, with an exuberant growth of underwood.
The music of almost every feathered songster that
frequents the woods of England is heard in this wild
spot ; but except the buzzing of flies that rise in crowds
from the copses, and the pleasant rippling of the stream,
no other sound meets the ear.

The old tree with its bleached and skeleton arms has
a fearful name, and stout of heart must the man be who
would pass within sight of it when the sun is set behind
the hill, and the trees cast their lengthened shadows on
the grass. It is called the 'haunted oak,' the 'spirit's
blasted tree,' or the 'hobgoblin's hollow tree,' and dismal
is the tale to which the name refers.

Howel Sele, whose sad history is associated with this
blasted oak, was lord of the wide domain which extends
around it for many miles. We know not whether his
heart was secretly inclined to espouse the faction of
Henry IV., or whether he loved a life of ease, and
preferred to dwell in his castle-hall, hoping that the
storm which threatened to overwhelm his country might
pass away. Certain it is that Owen Glendour thought
not well of him, and perhaps with reason. He came
not forth to assist in delivering his country from the

aggressions of a foreign enemy; some even said that he had been induced to desert her cause, and that he only waited for an opportunity to avow himself. Others, whispered, that he looked with a jealous eye on the generous Glendour; and that he feared not to speak of him as the sole leader of a desperate faction, who, if deprived of their head, had no other hope.

Glendour knew that such evil rumours were abroad, and it seemed as if he wished to set his kinsman at defiance; for having taken with him his chosen companion Madog, he set forth to drive the red deer from the forest brake, in the domains of the unbending lord of Nannau. But the lord of Nannau could not brook that his red deer should be thus vexed and driven, and when one of these noble animals crossed his path, closely pursued by the fiery Glendour with hound and horn, he rushed from the forest and summoned his cousin to single combat. It was a fatal one for Howel; he fell on the green sward, in the very place where all is now so verdurous and joyful, and his corpse was dragged by his enraged kinsman beneath the tree, whose bare and sapless branches and high top, bald with dry antiquity, whose gnarled and rugged trunk, and large projecting roots are almost fearful in their decay.

The tree was hollow at that time, and the companion of Glendour having, with his assistance, lifted the corpse of the unhappy chieftain from off the ground, dropped it within the oak. This was a ruthless deed, but the

natural gentleness of Owen Glendour had been perverted
by the scenes in which he mingled, and by the oppres-
sion that was exercised towards him. He saw only, in
the husband and the father who had fallen by his hand,
one, who, if he favoured not the cause of the usurper,
was yet indifferent to the welfare of his country. He,
therefore, sought not for him Christian burial, in con-
secrated ground.

Glendour could no longer tarry in the domains of the
murdered chieftain, for he knew how greatly Howel was
beloved, and that when the hour of his return was
passed, every glen and forest-path would be sought for
him. Calling to his companion, he hastened back to
his stronghold, Glyndwrdry, where, amid rocks and
waterfalls, and the howling of fierce winds, he passed a
few more unquiet years. The wretched day which
caused him to become a murderer, and deprived Nannau
of her lord, was one of anxiety and grief. Far and
wide did his vassals haste, now down the glen, now in
the depth of the still forest, now scouring over the wide
moor, and now making every rock resound with his
name. But in vain did they hurry along the forest
paths, or dash amid the torrent's roar, or scour over the
wide moor, echo alone answered to their loud shouts.
In vain did the sorrowing wife of Howel look out
through the gloom of evening, and listen for his foot-
steps ; and when the moon shone bright, and louder
sounded the wild torrent, and the whoop of the owl was

heard, did she pace her lonely chamber and strain her sight through the gathered mist, to see if he was coming.

The next day, and the next, did the vassals of Nannau renew their search. Again every glen was visited, and every forest-walk was traced and retraced ; the base, too, of every hill was carefully examined, lest the chieftain should have fallen from some height, which the creeping bramble and thickly-tangled underwood had concealed. But no trace of Howel was discovered.

Thus one year succeeded to another, and no tidings of the chieftain were received, till at length an armed horseman was seen to urge his weary steed up the hill that leads to Nannau, from the neighbouring town of Dolgelly. The rain fell fast, and the wind blew a perfect hurricane, but he seemed not to heed either the one or the other, or to spare the horse on which he rode. The vassals hastened to the castle-gate, and the lady looked anxiously from the window. Perhaps a faint hope flashed across her mind that the Lord of Nannau was returning. But it was not him, although the stranger brought tidings where he might be found. He told the lady that the enemy of her house was dead ; that he in dying, had conjured him to bring to her ear tidings of her husband, and to make known the dreadful mystery of his sudden disappearance. He then told his tale ; for it was Madoc, who came thus late, and he referred to the blasted oak in confirmation of the truth.

The vassals of Nannau hurried thither, and with them went Madoc, but he could not bear to see the bringing forth of him, whom he had helped to sepulchre within its trunk; he shrunk from witnessing the awful sight that was about to be revealed, and plunging into the forest was soon on the road to Dolgelly. The evening was far advanced when Madoc reached the castle, and now the night had closed in. The vassals worked by torchlight, for such was the lady's command, and their own eagerness confirmed it. Their strokes fell heavy on the trunk of the tree, which sounded hollow, and somewhat of a rattling was heard within, as if of iron and of bones. Some feared to continue, and truly it was solemn work, for the night was dark, and the wind exceeding loud, and the tree stood forth in its sepulchral whiteness, with its long skeleton-looking and bleached arms, which the lightning had riven. A few strokes more, and the horrid mystery was revealed. There stood the skeleton of Howell; his right hand grasped a rusty sword, and those who saw it, well remembered that it had often been wielded by their chieftain.

Queen Mary's Tower.

Oh! 'tis a strange unearthly sound,
When loud the raging wind rides round
This ruined home of other days;
The warrior's boast, the minstrel's praise !
For now the stately pile is low,
And rank the grass and nettles grow,
Where princes sat in regal state,
And bold retainers past the gate.—
The strong old gate, all broken now,
Twin'd with the ivy's matted bough.—M. R.

SUCH is Winfield castle; and its noble oak, the old oak which bears its name, stands within sight of the long suite of rooms where Mary Stuart passed nine years of her sad captivity; for even nine years, however passed, teaches many a heavy lesson. Much of grief and sorrow, and those strange reverses which only the great may feel in all their fulness and their bitterness, had been comprised in the short life of this unhappy princess, once the Queen of France, then of Scotland, but at length a prisoner, when she passed beneath the portcullis of Winfield castle. Other tales

of sorrow and endurance, but none more pitiable, were
connected with this old castle: its early history is lost in
the uncertainty of ages; no one knows who built it, or
why it stands in this wild spot, whether its origin be
Saxon or Danish; except that its first and oldest name
was given in commemoration of some forgotten vic-
tory.   Peverel of the Peak, erected the high tower, with
a portion of the walls, and successive chieftains added
to the structure, till at length the castle came to be
much spoken of for its size and strength.   Peverel's
tower still remains, with a part of the old building, but
that portion of it which more than any other awakens
images of bygone days, are the rooms of state, with a
small tower on the wall, where the captive queen re-
sided; tradition says that she used to spend much of her
time in summer on the roof of the tower, watching for
signals from Leonard Dacre, who made many attempts
to procure her liberation, either by force or stratagem.
But the vigilance of the Earl of Shrewsbury was not
readily eluded; and for nine long years did Mary inhabit
this stern fortress, and watch from her high tower for
succour that never came.

   Ruins are best seen in wintry weather, when storms and
thunder are abroad, and the woods are bare of leaves.
Such was the fourteenth of October, when some years
back, the narrator, saw for the first time, that dila-
pidated portion of Winfield castle.   The rain had been
exceeding heavy in the night, and the wind blew a per-

fect hurricane, making the tall trees groan and sway, beneath its fury, and driving the autumn leaves in shoals upon the ground. But the rain had ceased, and the loud wind was still, except when it came in gusts, moaning over the wide heath, and around the ancient castle, with that wailing sound which is heard only in places where men have dwelt, as if singing the wild requiem of departed greatness. The skirt of the heavy storm-cloud was seen retreating in the west, with its grey windy banners; while, on high, rolling masses of dark clouds were following swiftly, as if they feared to be left behind. Now they were no more seen; clouds, of a still somewhat stormy character, succeeded them, hurrying across the heavens, and changing as they passed, at one moment dark and threatening, at another light and fleecy; while at intervals the blue sky appeared, and the sun broke forth gloriously, causing the earth to look as if it smiled from some internal consciousness of delight.

The view from the old tree accorded well with the stormy aspect of the heavens on that day. Full in front rises the stately keep, with its broken battlements and rusted portcullis, its strong iron-bossed oaken door, rusted also on its hinges, brown and broken, with large spaces, showing the desolate and grass-grown area within. To the right of the keep extends a high wall, flanked with a round tower, and then a long sweep of wall, without windows, separated by a strong jutting out from another wall, wherein are the state apartments which Mary occupied.

Here stands the tower which bears her name, and from amid a mass of ruins at the base springs up a beautiful ash, which rises to the highest story, and waves before her window.   Well might that tree be called Mary's Ash, for the ash is the Venus of the forest, the most graceful of all trees, and she was the loveliest of her kind.   It seems to grow there, a living thing, where all else tells of death and ruin; a beautiful and appropriate memorial of one who was the fairest among women, in the days of her sojourning.   Unlike the oak of Winfield, which stands in its strength, rugged and embossed, with upheaved roots and strong boughs, fitted to resist the storms of ages ; standing, perhaps, when Peverel of the Peak, leaving his stronghold on the summit of the castle-rock, raised here his tower in a fairer spot, deep forested, with green fields, and ample hunting grounds.   When, too, successive chieftains enlarged the bold structure, and presided with all the pomp and splendour of feudal magnificence.   But the ash had no root within the soil when Mary lived here,—when the Earl of Shrewsbury, his stately dame, her maidens, and his men-at-arms, inhabited the castle. The ash sprung up since Mary went away, and now its leafless branches wave before the window where she used to watch and weep.

The Chesnut of Tortworth.

When Eva, the gentle one, came,
  And sat down in my ample shade;
And with her was that noble Thane,
  The lov'd one of the Saxon maid;

I call'd to the rustling breeze,
  That my boughs might their homage pay;
While the joyous birds sang from the trees,
  And the soaring lark warbled his lay.—M. R.

THE great Chesnut of Tortworth stood where now it stands, far back as the reign of John, at which period it bore the name that still distinguishes it among trees of the same species. It was then in all its grandeur and luxuriance, and its noble branches cast a deep and lengthened shade upon the waste beneath, for grass and flowers do not readily vegetate under the shadow of the chesnut. But the deer of the forest resorted thither to feed on the nuts, when shaken from the boughs by autumn winds; thither, also, troops of wild hogs, which the Saxons used to pasture in the woods, would gather beside the tree, and listen for the dropping of the kernels that fell in their ripeness to the ground.

Had Salvator Rosa been living when the great chesnut was in its prime, he would have braved the dangers both of land and sea to have studied its magnificent proportions, for this is the tree which graces all his landscapes; it flourished in the mountains of Calabria, where he painted, and there he observed it in all its forms, breaking and disposing of it, in a variety of beautiful shapes, as the exigences of his compositions required. But Salvator Rosa was not then living, nor, perhaps, his ancestors for many generations; neither was the art of painting developed in England; that beautiful art, which transmits to canvas the glow of an evening sky, and the effects of foliage when shaken by the wind; which embodies, within the space of a few inches, an extent of many miles, with mingled wood and flood, bold headlands and mountains fading in the distance, or crowded cities, with their palaces and schools. Even the Bayeux tapestry, which chronicled, in after years, events connected with civil history and domestic misery, presented merely an ungraceful portraiture of passing events.

The tree had attained nearly to its altitude at that period of England's sorrows, when the fierce Penda carried war and desolation through some of her fairest provinces. At this time, also, his son, being appointed Governor of Mercia, resided with his wife, Eva, at Glocester, in the centre of his dominions, where many persecuted persons, who fled from the sword of Penda, were secretly protected and relieved, for Eva was a

Christian, and her husband inclined to her faith. Glou-
cester, where they held their court, was a place of great
antiquity. It was one of the twenty-eight cities which
the Britons erected, previous to their conquest by the
Romans, and was called Caer-Glou, or Caer-Gloyw,
which signified, in their language, the bright or splendid
town, from its situation on an eminence at the termina-
tion of the flat and marshy part of the kingdom of
Mercia, and being well watered with an ample river.

Wolfere presided over the dominions which his father
confided to his care, with equal wisdom and considera-
tion ; but within the range of the highest window of his
palace, grievous sights were witnessed at one time, by
those who had the hardihood to look for them. A dread-
ful battle was fought in the neighbourhood of Corinium,
at about twelve miles distant, between the fierce king, for
whom Wolfere ruled, and the King of Wessex. Corinium
was much fallen from its ancient grandeur : it had been,
in former times, the seat of arts and elegance ; Roman
generals lived there, and there Constantine occasionally
resided; but war and time had greatly changed its once
royal aspect, though still a considerable city, and having
within its precincts a store of goods and cattle. Penda
desired to possess them, and the hard victory which he
gained before the walls gave the inhabitants an earnest of
the calamities that awaited them. The consequences of
this great victory were severely felt in the kingdom of
Wessex, and again, throughout the wide expanse of the

Cotswold Hills, and among the beautiful vales of Mercia, were acted those scenes of misery, which the youths of that day had shuddered to hear beside the blazing hearth-stone, when narrated in the winter tales of their grandfathers.

The victory which Penda had gained, within sight of his son's palace at Gloucester, was succeeded by the fall of the brave Oswold, near Oswestry, in Shropshire. The kingdom of Bernicia was added by his death to the already extensive dominions of the conqueror, and with the increase of his territories, increased also the sufferings of the Christians, whom he persecuted with unwearied malignity. Penda was born a pagan, and as such he passed the period of his youth and middle age. According to the custom of his country, he worshipped images of wood and stone, and joined devoutly in all the unhallowed rites which had been established by his Saxon ancestors; like them he believed that demons of good or ill presided over the fields and groves, and he sought to obtain the favour of the one, and to conciliate the other, by such observances and propitiations as the priesthood had enjoined. To them he was devoutly attached, and his temper being naturally inclined to seriousness, somewhat too, unyielding, with a strong bias to religion, he sought to extirpate the Christian faith, which had been represented to him as tending equally to overthrow the altars of his ruthless deities, with the throne itself.

But the Saviour, whose disciples he thus ignorantly

persecuted, refused not, on his behalf, the prayers of one who ceased not to supplicate that he might become a sharer in the hopes and blessings of which she knew the value. This was Eva, who has been already mentioned as the wife of his son, Wolfere, the governor of Mercia. Men of the present generation, those even who live where she once lived, have heard little concerning her. Historians speak rather of crimes and sorrows; they chronicle what the great adversary of mankind has achieved to make nations miserable; the life spent in quiet duty, the lifting up of the heart in secret prayer, are no themes for them. But the memorial of Eva is in heaven, her record is on high, and there is reason to believe that she was allowed to witness the softening of that rugged temper, which had occasioned such a variety of wretchedness—to hear, also, that Penda allowed the preaching of Christianity in his dominions nearly two years before his death. It was even said that he was baptized by Bishop Aiden, with Sigebert, King of the East-Angles.

Eva died in good old age, after presiding for more than thirty years over the nunnery of St Peter's, at Gloucester. She retired thither on the death of her husband, and greatly benefited the abbey to which it was attached, by causing the revenues to be increased, and by obtaining the confirmation of former donations. With her terminated the office of lady Abbess, during the cruel war which succeeded, between Egbert and the King of Mercia, when the nuns were forced to depart, and the abbey became deso-

late.   The roof which had sheltered the remains of for-
mer Abbesses, of Eilburg, who governed the nunnery, both
religiously and prudently, for more than half a century,
and of Kyneburg, the widow of Elred, King of Northum-
berland, was thrown open to the winds of heaven, and
nothing remained of its former splendour but walls black
with smoke, and a few broken effigies.

Neither Wolfere, nor his wife Eva, anticipated that
such would be the fate of the noble abbey which the piety
of former kings had founded, and which the governor of
Mercia sought to enlarge and beautify, because Eva
loved to worship there.   The future is in mercy veiled
from the eyes of men ; they could not bear to contem-
plate events that are often close at hand, for though
strength is promised for the day of sorrow, it is not given
before that sorrow comes.   Eva went, as she was wont,
on every holy day, to offer prayers, and to present her
gifts within the hallowed walls of St Peter's Abbey, and
Wolfere continued to embellish the noble city that was
confided to his care, by causing many spacious buildings
to be erected both for ornament and use.   The city had
suffered greatly in former wars, and he not only rebuilt
such portions of the walls as had been broken down, but
so enlarged and adorned it, that it was soon spoken of as
one of the finest cities in the Heptarchy.   Great hospi-
tality was also exercised at his court, and many found a
shelter there, whose homes had been destroyed in the
rage of civil discord.

The presidency of Wolfere, therefore, over the king-dom of Mercia; the noble acts which he achieved in beautifying and enlarging the city of Caer-Glou, and the quiet, unassuming labours of his wife, Eva, were cotemporary with the Chesnut of Tortworth when it first attained its high standing among forest-trees. It may be, that the venerable ruin, whose decaying trunk is still surmounted by a few verdant branches, was looked upon in its day of pride, by Wolfere and Eva. Tortworth was mentioned, in the time of John, as an ancient place, and the tree of which we speak was called the Great Chesnut. It grew within the garden-wall of the old mansion, and we have no reason to believe that the site on which it stood, had been recently reclaimed from the forest.

𝕮𝖆𝖑𝖑𝖆𝖈𝖊'𝖘 𝕺𝖆𝖐.

The old Memorial tree is down ;
   But its stirring legend still lives on :
A tale of grief and withering woe,
    Of tears that ceased long ago.—M. R.

THE noble Oak of Ellerslie sheltered the birth-place of
Wallace. Centuries have passed since then, and now it
stands in the centre of a small common, time-worn and
reft of all its greatness, a magnificent ruin; although,
within the memory of man, its ample branches extended
over a Scotch acre of ground. Wallace, and the children
of the village, used to play beneath its shelter: they
would gather acorns for cups and balls, and rest on the
green sward when they were hot and weary.

A poet, perhaps, would tell you that the patriarchal
tree loved to look down on the young " wee things," whose
remotest ancestors—precursors, it may be, of a thousand
generations, to the period concerning which we speak—
had dwelt beside it ; that it liked to screen them from the
noonday heat ; and that, when a sudden shower, driving
furiously from off the hills, made the fondlings haste
beneath its branches, it kept off the heavy rain-drops that
they might not harm the merry crowd. Certain it is that

the village children liked best to play beneath the shade
of the old oak, and that their parents knew where to seek
for the young truants, when they had wandered from
school or home. We can all enter into the feelings of
children, for we have been children ourselves; we can
remember how the primrose and the cowslip, although
the gathering of them often gained for us both colds and
chidings; the nest of the hedge-sparrow, or the coming
forth of the white thorn, were things of vast importance;
what delight the finding of them imparted, and how every
new object powerfully excited the young mind, because
they had all, and each, the charm of novelty   We know,
also, that as months and years pass on, somewhat of care
begins to steal across all this joyousness, as the shadow of
a passing cloud obscures a sunny landscape; that the cares
of every day occurrence—the difficulty of finding bread
for a large young family—the father's weariness after a
day of labour, and the anxious feelings of the mother, are
soon shared in by children.   They feel more than
any one imagines who does not vividly remember what
his or her feelings have been in very early life, although
the feelings were not, perhaps, depressed by circumstances
of equal trial.   Time goes on, and it is not only home
sorrows that engross the mind; if the days in which they
live, are stormy, and men speak of their country's
wrongs, the striplings aspire to aid in seeking redress;
and the ardour by which their fathers are excited,
is reflected in them with double vividness.   Thus

it was at the period when Wallace lived. The
thoughts of all were much engrossed by the terrible
condition of the country, and the once playful children,
who used to assemble beneath the Oak of Ellerslie, now
grown up to boyhood, heard from their fathers that the
English army was advancing with all speed towards the
border land.   Edward led them on, but he had no right
to the crown of Scotland.   Alexander III., who had filled
till lately the now vacant throne, and who had espoused the
sister of Edward, most probably inherited, after a period
of eight hundred years, and through a succession of
males, the sceptre of all the Scottish princes; of those,
who, although the country had been continually exposed
to such factions and convulsions as are incident to all
barbarous, and to many civilized nations, had governed
her rocks and fastnesses, from a period whose commence-
ment is lost in the obscurity of ages.   But the king was
dead; he had fallen from his horse at Kinghorn, and the
maid of Norway, as she was termed, daughter of Eric, her
king, and his own fair daughter Margaret, was the only re-
presentative of the Scottish dynasty. Alexander had wisely
caused her to be recognized by the states of Scotland, as
the lawful heir of the kingdom, and though an infant and
a foreigner, she was immediately received as such.   Mar-
garet was accordingly proclaimed queen, and the disposi-
tions which had been made against the event of Alexander's
death appeared so just and prudent, that no disorders, as
might naturally be apprehended, ensued in the kingdom.

Five guardians, the Bishops of St. Andrew's and Glasgow, the Earls of Fife and Bucan, and James Steward, were appointed to take charge of the young princess. These men, who were distinguished for their talents and integrity, entered peaceably upon the administration, and the infant queen, under the protection of Edward, her great uncle, and Eric her father, set forth on her voyage towards Scotland. But either the fatigue attendant on an expedition by sea, or else, in her young mind, grief at leaving the companions of her childhood, affected her health; she suddenly became ill, and died on the passage.

There were sad hearts in Scotland, when the heavy tidings reached her of the young queen's death; and when it was heard by those who met at evening around the oak of Ellerslie, they looked anxiously one upon the other, for they knew not what to say; it seemed to them that all hope for the weal of Scotland was about to be extinguished. They knew that Edward was both powerful and crafty; that having lately, by force of arms, brought Wales under subjection, he had designed, by the marriage of Margaret with his eldest son, to unite the whole island under one monarchy. With this view he had dispatched an embassy to the states of Scotland, when the late king died, and the proposal being favourable to the happiness and security of the kingdom, it was readily assented to. It was even agreed by the five guardians, that their young sovereign should be educated at the English court, while they at the same time, stipulated that Scotland should enjoy her ancient liberties and customs, and that in case the prince and Margaret should die without children, the crown of Scotland should revert to the next heir. The projected marriage promised well, but the sudden death of the young princess left only a dismal prospect for the kingdom. No breaking-out among the people immediately ensued, for the regency was sufficiently powerful to keep the crown from sudden spoliation. It was otherwise in the course of a short time, for several pretenders laid claim to the vacant throne. The posterity of William, King of Scotland, the prince who was taken prisoner by Henry II., being extinct on the death of Margaret, the crown devolved by natural right to the representatives of David, Earl of Huntingdon, brother to William, whose male line being also extinct, left the succession open to the descendants of his daughters. John Baliol repre- sented his maternal ancestor Margaret, one of the three daughters of the Earl of Huntingdon, married to Alan, Lord of Galloway; Robert Bruce of Annandale, his mother Isabella; and John Hastings, the lady Adama, who espoused Henry Lord Hastings. This last pretended that the kingdom of Scotland, like other inheritances, was divisible among the three co-heiresses of the Earl of Huntingdon, and that he, in right of his mother, was entitled to a third. Baliol and Bruce spurned at the thought of dismembering the country, while each asserted the superiority of his own claim.

E

Baliol was sprung from the elder branch, Bruce was one degree nearer the common stock; if the principle of representation was regarded, the former had the better claim ; if consanguinity was considered, the latter was entitled to the preference. The sentiments of men were divided, all the nobility took part with one or other of the claimants, and the people implicitly followed their leaders. The different claimants themselves had great power and numerous retainers in Scotland, and each thought himself secure of gaining the Scottish throne. The danger which threatened the country was therefore iminent. The most thoughtless saw that a furious civil war would infallibly occur, unless some plan could be devised for adverting so terrible a calamity ; and men, high in power, of all parties, and themselves secretly inclining either to Baliol, or Bruce, or Hastings, resolved, if possible, to lay aside their mutual differences, and to agree upon some measure for preserving the public peace.

Many and lengthened were the discussions which they held. The best and most obvious method of averting the threatened calamity, was to prevail upon two of the contending parties to lay aside their mutual claims. But this they would not do ; each saw, or fancied that he saw, the crown of Scotland within his grasp, and he cared not if it was gained at the cost of a civil war. Another expedient then occurred to those who sat in council for the public good. This was the submitting

of the question to the judgment of King Edward. For
such a measure they had many precedents. The
English king and his barons, in the preceding reign, had
endeavoured to settle their differences by a reference
to the King of France, and the integrity of that monarch
had prevented any of the bad effects which might other-
wise have ensued. The kings of France and Arragon,
and afterwards other princes, had appealed in like
manner to Edward's arbitration, and he had acquitted
himself with honour in his decisions. The parlia-
ment of Scotland, therefore, wishing if possible to pre-
vent the misery attendant on civil discord, and allured
by the great reputation of the English monarch, as well
as by the amicable correspondence which had existed
between the kingdoms, agreed in making a reference to
Edward. Men of probity were chosen as deputies, and
among these, Frazer, Bishop of St. Andrews, left his
quiet home on the plains of Fife, at a short distance from
the German ocean, to undertake a long and perilous ex-
pedition to the English court. They remembered that
her monarch would have stood in the relationship of a
father to their young queen, they had heard much
concerning his integrity and honour, and how he had
kept peace in France and Arragon, and they flattered
themselves that he would now interfere in the affairs
of a sister kingdom, with such authority as none of
the competitors would dare to withstand.

Hope revived in Scotland, and many fondly trusted

that the heavy cloud which had begun to settle on her mountains, and threatened to deluge her plains with wretchedness, would yet pass away.

Men often possess a high character for virtue, because they have no temptation to act wrong. In the case of France and Arragon, the remoteness of the states, the great power of their respective princes, and the little interest which Edward had on either side, induced him to acquit himself with strict impartiality in his decisions. It was not so in the present case, and the temptation was too strong for the English monarch to resist. He secretly purposed to lay hold of the present favourable opportunity, and if not to create, at least to revive, his claim of a feudal supremacy over Scotland ; a claim which had hitherto lain in the deepest obscurity, and which, if it had ever been an object of attention, or had been so much as suspected, would have prevented the Scottish barons from choosing him as umpire. Passing by the archives of the empire, which, had his claim been real, must have afforded numerous records of homage done by the Scottish princes, he caused the monasteries to be ransacked for old chronicles and histories of bygone days, and from these every passage was transcribed which seemed to favour his pretensions. The amount of all such transcripts, when taken collectively, merely went to show that the Scots had occasionally been defeated by the English, and had concluded peace on disadvantageous terms. It was proved, indeed, that when the King of Scotland, William, was

taken prisoner at the battle of Alnwic, he was con-
strained, for the recovery of his liberty, to swear fealty
to the victor. But even this faint claim to feudal su-
periority on one side, of submission on the other, was
done away by Richard II. That monarch being desirous
to conciliate the friendship of the Scottish king, before
his departure for the Holy Land, renounced the homage,
which he said, in express terms, had been extorted by his
father.

The commissioners soon perceived with dismay, that
all which they could urge against the pretensions of the
English monarch, were utterly unavailing. They heard,
too, that a royal commission had been issued for the fitting
out of a great armament, and intelligence quickly followed
that the army was on its march to Scotland.

Edward and his men-at-arms, reached Norham Castle,
on the southern banks of the Tweed, where he insiduously
invited the Scottish parliament, and all the competitors to
attend him, in order to determine the cause which had
been referred to his arbitration. They came, but not
on equal terms, for the English king brought with him a
large body of warlike men, ready to do his bidding;
while the parliament found themselves betrayed into a
situation in which it was impossible to make any stand,
for the liberty and independence of their country. One
anxious year for Scotland passed on, while Edward pre-
tended, impartially, to examine the claims of the various
competitors, for nine others had now started. Having

thus gained time for the furtherance of his ambitious view, he pronounced sentence in favour of Baliol. Baliol was, therefore, placed on the throne of Scotland, with the shadow merely of royal authority, for many and humiliating were the concessions which Edward required of the seeming king. They were such as even his mild and yielding disposition could not brook, and at length, taking advantage of a favourable juncture, he resolved to make a desperate effort for the restoration of his rights.

Rumours were soon afloat that an English army was rapidly advancing, and scarcely was the intelligence received, than it was also heard that some of the most powerful among the Scottish nobles, with Robert Bruce, the father and the son, and the Earls of March and Angus, foreseeing the ruin of their country from the concurrence of intestine divisions, and a foreign invasion, had submitted to the English king. Other rumours followed, fraught with distress for Scotland. Some related that the English troops had actually crossed the Tweed without opposition, at Coldstream; others that Baliol, having procured for himself, and for his nation, Pope Celestine's dispensation from former oaths, renounced the homage which he had done to England, and was already at the head of a great army. Some spoke what they believed, others as they wished; but there was little ground for exultation as respected the movements of the Scotch king. Instead of bringing into the field any effective force, with which to oppose the encroachments

of the English, he was constrained to hear of their con-
tinual successes. The castle of Roxborough was taken;
Edinburgh and Stirling opened their gates to the enemy.
All the southern portions of the country were readily
subdued, and Edward, still better to reduce the northern,
whose rocks and fastnesses afforded some security, sent
for a strong reinforcement of Welch and Irish. These
men, being accustomed to a desultory kind of warfare,
were best fitted to pursue the fugitive Scots into the
recesses of their glens and mountains. The quiet valleys
and the upland solitudes, which had been untrodden by
stranger steps for ages, were visited in consequence, and
hostile men sat down beneath the shade of the old Oak
of Ellerslie.

The spirit of the nation was broken at this period.
Edward marched northward to Aberdeen and Elgin,
without meeting an enemy. No Scotchman approached,
but to pay him homage. Even the bold chieftains, ever
refractory to their own princes, and averse to the restraint
of laws, endeavoured to prevent the devastation of their
mountain homes, by giving the usurper early proofs of
obedience. The bards alone stood firm; they sung to
the music of their harps the high and moving strains
which, in ancient days, had roused those who heard them
to a pitch of the wildest enthusiasm.

Scotland being thus reduced to a state of seeming
dependence, the English forces generally repassed the
Tweed, although strong garrisons remained in every castle of

importance. They had carried with them that ancient stone, on which, from the remotest period either of history or of tradition, the Kings of Scotland received the rite of inauguration. They believed, on the faith of an ancient prophecy, that wherever this stone was placed, their nation should always govern; it was also treasured up in the minds of men, among their fondest traditions, that the day would come when one of Scottish birth should rule over England. Scone was no longer permitted to retain the true palladium of their monarchy; it was proudly carried off, and placed in the palace of Westminster. There was seeming tranquillity throughout Scotland on the day of its removal from the ancient church at Scone, but the hearts of all who saw it pass, or who heard of its removal, burned within them. The deed was spoken off throughout all Scotland. Men heard of it in the remotest parts; the chieftain in his castle-hall, the peasant in his highland hut; they were constrained to smother the indignation that glowed within them, yet they secretly awaited a favourable opportunity to assert the independence of their country. Baliol, too, was carried, a prisoner, to London; his great seal was broken, and when, after the lapse of two years' confinement in the Tower, he was restored to liberty, it was with the harsh condition that he should submit to a voluntary banishment in France. Thither, accordingly, he retired, and died in a private station.

Scotland, meanwhile, was in a deplorable condition. Her king was powerless, and the administration of the country was in the hands of rapacious men —of Ormesby, who had been appointed justiciary by Edward; and Cressingham the treasurer. The latter had no other object than to amass money by rapine and injustice; the former was notorious for the rigour and severity of his temper: and both, treating the Scots as a conquered people, made them sensible too early of the grievous servitude into which they had fallen.

William Wallace was now grown to man's estate. His young companions had grown up also, and the group of merry children, that had played under the old Oak of Ellerslie, were now thoughtful men and women; for the troubles of the days in which they lived, made even the young grow thoughtful. The old men wished that they could wield their good weapons as in days of yore, for then, they said, stout-hearts that beat beneath the highland tartan, would not have tamely yielded to become the vassals of proud England. Their country had once held, they said, a station among the kingdoms of the earth, but now she was fallen and degraded; their king was taken from them, and mercenary men oppressed the people with heavy taxes. Thus spoke the old men of Ellerslie, and such were the thoughts of thousands throughout the land.

Wallace and his young companions, actuated by that enthusiasm which the oft-told tale of ancient valour and present degradation, was calculated to inspire; excited also by the conversation of strangers from the north, and stimulated by the present favourable aspect of affairs, (for the English troops were mostly withdrawn to their own country,) resolved to attempt the desperate enterprise of delivering their native land from the dominion of foreigners. Wallace was well-fitted for the purpose. He was a man of gigantic strength, his nerves were braced by a youth of hardihood and exercise; he possessed like-wise ability to bear fatigue, and the utmost severity of weather. Nor were his mental characteristics less remarkable. He was endowed with heroic courage, with disinterested magnanimity, and incredible patience. The ill conduct of an English officer had provoked him beyond endurance, and finding himself obnoxious to the severity of the administration, he fled into the woods which surrounded his once happy home, and invited to his banner all those whom their crimes, or misfortunes, or avowed hatred to the English, had reduced to a like necessity.

Beginning with small attempts, in which he was uni-formly successful, Wallace gradually proceeded to momen-tous enterprises. He was enabled by his knowledge of the country to ensure a safe retreat whenever it was needful to hide himself among the morasses and the mountains; and it was said, that he once concealed him-self, with three hundred of his men, among the branches of the aged oak, beneath which he had played in child-hood. But Ellerslie was not long a place for him, though he still loved to linger in its beautiful retreats. They were too well known to those who sought to take his life, for the village in which his parents lived, lay not far distant from one of the strong castles, in which the English had a garrison. He went, therefore, to Torwood, in the county of Stirling, and made the giant oak which stood there his head-quarters. It was believed to be the largest tree that ever grew in Scotland. Centuries were chronicled on its venerable trunk, and tradition traced it to the era of the Druids. The remains of a circle of unhewn stone were seen within its precincts, and near it was an ancient causeway. Wallace often slept in its hollow trunk during his protracted struggles against the tyranny of Edward, with many of his officers, for the cavity afforded an ample space.

The old Oak of Torwood was to him a favourite haunt; perhaps it was associated in his mind with the one he had left at Ellerslie: but other, and far-off scenes, were often the theatre of his most heroic actions, when, having ensured a retreat from the close pursuit of the enemy, he collected his dispersed associates, and unexpectedly appearing in another quarter, surprised and routed the unwary English. Such actions soon gained for him the applause and admiration of his countrymen. They seemed to vindicate the nation from the ignominy into which it had fallen, by its tame submission to a foreign yoke; and although no man of rank ventured as yet to join his party, he was universally spoken of, by all who desired the independence of their country, as one who promised to realise their most ardent wishes.

Cambuskenneth, on the opposite banks of the impetuous Forth, became the theatre of a decisive victory, which seemed about to deliver Scotland from the oppression of a foreign yoke. Wallace, at this time, stood alone with a band of faithful men, who adhered to him in all his struggles and vicissitudes. Earl Warrenne, whom the king had originally appointed Governor of Scotland, on the abdication of Baliol, which office he had relinquished conditionally, from ill health, had crossed the border-land with an army of forty thousand men; he now sought by the celerity of his armament, and his march, to compensate for his past negligence in the appointment of Cressingham and Ormsby. Advancing with incredible rapidity, he suddenly entered Annandale, and came up with the Scots at Ervine, before their forces were collected, and before they had put themselves in a posture of defence. Many of the nobles being thus unexpectedly placed in a great dilemma, thought to save their estates by submitting to Earl Warrenne. But Wallace, nothing daunted, awaited his further progress on the banks of the Forth. Victory declared in his favour, and the wreck of the invading army, being driven from the field, made its escape to England.

Had Wallace been permitted to retain the dignity of regent or guardian of the kingdom, under the captive Baliol, all might yet have been well with Scotland. The elevation of the patriot chief, though purchased by so great merit, and such eminent services, was not, however, agreeable to the nobility; they could not brook that a private gentleman should be raised above them by his rank, still less by his wisdom and reputation. Wallace himself, sensible of their jealousies, and fearing for the safety of his country, resigned his authority, and retained only the command over that small troop, many of whom had been his companions in their boyhood days, whose parents had dwelt with his, beside the Oak of Ellerslie, and who refused to follow the standard of any other leader. Nobly, therefore, did he consent to serve under the Steward of Scotland, and Cummin of Badenoch, into whose hands the great chieftains had devolved the guardianship of their country. Meanwhile another army crossed the Forth, and the two commanders proposed to await its coming up on the banks of Falkirk river. Wallace was also there with his chosen band. In this battle the Scots were worsted, and it seemed to those who heard of it, that the ruin of Scotland was inevitable.

Wallace, although he continually exposed himself in the hottest of the fray, was enabled by his military skill and great presence of mind, to keep his men together. Retiring behind the Carron, he marched along the banks of the river, which protected him from the enemy. The country on either side was wild and picturesque; the yellow gorse was in blossom, and the

continuous flowers of the heath seemed to shed a purple
light upon the mountains. It was then in all its beauty,
for even the sternest scenes are beautiful when decked in
their summer glory, when gay flowers grow upon the
rocks, and birds and butterflies sport among them. The
heavens above were clear, and the shadows of flying
clouds seemed to set the plain country in motion; where
the grass grew wild and high, it looked as if innumerable
pigmies were passing swiftly beneath the blades, and
causing them to rock to and fro with their rapid move-
ment. But not a sound was heard, except the heavy
tread of weary men, and the murmur of the river over
its pebbly bed.

Young Bruce, who had given many proofs of aspiring
genius, and who had served hitherto in the English
army, appeared on the opposite bank of the river. While
standing there, and thinking, perhaps, as men are apt to
think, when the loveliness of creation is presented in
striking contrast to scenes of ruin and desolation, he
observed the Scottish chief, who was distinguished as
well by his majestic port, as by the intrepid activity of
his behaviour. Calling out to him, he demanded a short
conference, and having represented to Wallace the fruit-
less and ruinous enterprise in which he was engaged,
he endeavoured to bend his ardent spirit to submission.
He represented the almost hopeless condition of the
country, the prevailing factions among the people, and
the jealousy of the chiefs. He spoke concerning the

wisdom and martial character of Edward, and how impossible it was that a weak state, deprived of its head, could long maintain such an unequal warfare. He told him, that if the love of his country was his motive for persevering, his obstinacy tended to prolong her woes; if he carried his views to personal aggrandisement and ambition, he might remember from past experience, that the proud nobles who constituted the aristocracy of Scotland, had already refused to submit to personal merit, although the elevation to which that merit attained had been won by the greatest privations, and by the consummate skill which had gained for them the hard-earned victory of Cambuskenneth.

Wallace was not slow to answer. He told young Bruce, that if he had acted as the champion of his country, it was solely because no leader had arisen, beneath whose banner he could lead on his faithful men. Why was not Bruce himself that leader? He had noble birth, and strength; he was in the vigour of his days, and yet, although uniting personal merit to dignity of family, he had been induced to desert the post which Heaven had assigned him. He told him that the Scots, possessed of such a head, would gladly assemble to his standard; that the proud nobles would submit to him, because he was of more exalted birth than any of them, being himself of royal descent; and that even now, though many brave, and some greatly distinguished men, had fallen on the battle-field at no great distance, and it seemed as if all hope as respects the future weal of Scotland was about to be extinguished; yet, if the noble youth to whom he spoke would but arouse himself, he might oppose successfully the power and abilities of Edward. Wallace urged him further to consider, that the Most High rarely offered a more glorious prize before the view either of virtue or ambition, than the acquisition of a crown, with the defence of national independence. That for his own part, while life remained, he should regard neither his own ease, nor yet the hardships to which he was exposed; that Scotland was dearer to him than the closest ties that entwine themselves around a brave man's heart, and that he was determined, as far as in him lay, to prolong, not her misery, but her independence, and to save her if possible from receiving the chains of a haughty victor. Bruce felt that what he said was true. From that moment he repented of his engagement with Edward, and opening his eyes to the honourable path, which the noble-minded Wallace had pointed out to him, he secretly determined to embrace the cause, however desperate, of his oppressed country.

Armies met again; other battles followed, and for two miserable years did the Scots and English fight hand to hand for the liberty or subjugation of Scotland. Edward at length triumphed, and Wallace became his prisoner. The boy of Ellerslie, he, who in after life thought only to preserve his country from spoliation; who was determined,

amid the general defection, the abrogation of laws and cus-
toms, and the razing of all monuments of antiquity, still to
maintain her independence, was betrayed into Edward's
hands, by a false friend, whom he had made acquainted with
the place of his retreat. He was carried in chains to London,
to be tried as a rebel and a traitor, though he had never
made submission, nor sworn fealty to England, and to be
executed on Tower Hill.

The old Oak of Ellerslie is still standing, and young
children play beneath its shade; the birds fly in and out,
and around it the life and business of husbandry proceeds,
as if neither grief nor death, had ever visited the beautiful
hills and dales that lie around.

More than five centuries have passed away since
young Wallace played with his companions beside the
tree, and a few short years, subtracted from that period,
since he took shelter with many of his playmates, when
grown up to manhood, among its ample branches. But
though long since barbarously executed, and though his
bones might not be laid to rest in the land which he sought
to save, he is not forgotten in the hallowed spot—the birth-
place of his parents—which he loved above all others. The
children of the village are still taught to lisp his name,
and are carried to hear of him beneath his own old tree.
All his favourite haunts by glen or burn, or up the moun-
tain-side, are fondly traced by the young men and
maidens when their work is done. Here, they say, he
used to sit and listen to the strain of the pibroch, and

from off the margin of the little stream he gathered flowers in his days of childhood. Yonder are the mountains, through the secret passes of which he used to conduct his small company of valiant men, when the storm of war gathered dense and dark, and from which he rushed like a mountain-torrent on the enemies of his country. Close at hand, say they, and extending even to the verge of the common on which stands the village of Ellerslie, are a few trees of the ancient wood, which often served for a hiding-place during his rapid alternations of advance and of retreat, and when in the small beginnings, which suited best with his youth—with the youth, too, of his companions—he gave good earnest of what his single arm might have effected, if secret jealousies and discordant counsels had not undermined his best concerted plans.

THE NUT TREE OR ROSOMONES GRAVE.

Oh many a one that weeps alone,
And whom the stern world brushes by,
Has friends whom kings might proudly own,
Though all unseen by mortal eye.—M.R.

"Away with that unseemly object!" said the stern St. Hugh, bishop of Lincoln, to the sisters of Godstow Nunnery, when he came in the course of visitation to their quiet dwelling among the rich meadows of Evenlod. "Away with that unseemly object! the hearse of one who was a Magdalen, is not a fitting spectacle for a quire of nuns to contemplate, nor is the front of the holy altar a proper place for such an exhibition."

The sisters dared not refuse, and the coffin which contained the remains of Fair Rosamond was removed to the church-yard. But they said among themselves, that the stern bishop needed not to have thus harshly judged, for Rosamond had lived among them for many years, in the utmost innocence and seclusion. They knew too, for so tradition tells, though the truth could not then be safely spoken, that poor Rosamond did not deserve the harsh aspersions of St. Hugh. It was believed that King Henry had married her in early life, but secretly, and without such witnesses as might avail, to have her constituted queen of England. Henry himself, when driven nearly to distraction by the rebellion of his acknowledged sons, spoke unadvisedly certain words, that confirmed the belief of the simple-hearted nuns. He said to one of the sons of Rosamond, who met him at the head of an armed company, "Thou art my legitimate son; the rest have no claim on me."[*]

Rosamond was told, most probably by the queen herself, of King Henry's conduct, for the queen, having seen him walking one day in the pleasure-grounds at Woodstock, with the end of a ball of silk attached to his spurs, and wondering greatly at the circumstance, resolved to follow him. She took up the ball, and when he went away, she followed warily, the silk meanwhile unwinding, till at length he suddenly disappeared in a thicket belonging to the celebrated labyrinth of Woodstock. The queen went no further, and kept the matter to herself. She, however, took advantage of his absence on a distant journey, and having threaded the mazes of the labyrinth, she began searching the thicket into which the king had disappeared. Finding a low door carefully concealed, the queen caused it to be forced

[*] Lingard.

open, and passing on with a beating heart through a
long, winding, subterraneous passage, she emerged again
into the open air, and following on a little further, she
discovered a lodge, situated in the most retired part of
the forest.   Beautiful trees grew round, with a spacious
garden, and a bower, in which a young lady was
seen busily engaged in embroidery.   This isolated
fact records merely the circumstance which led to the
finding of Fair Rosamond by Queen Eleanor; it speaks,
not of the bitter misery of the one, nor the distress
occasioned to the other, nor, most probably, the making
known by Rosamond, in the first moment of her dismay,
that she believed herself the wife of the man who had
entailed such wretchedness upon her.   But whatever
might have passed at that interview, its result was, the
retiring of Fair Rosamond from her secret bower to the
nunnery of Godstow, where she passed twenty years of
her weary life, and died when she was forty years of
age, in " the high odour of sanctity."   Her grave
remained unclosed, according to the fashion of the times,
but a sort of temporary covering, somewhat resembling
a tent, was raised immediately above it.   The coffin and
the tent were both before the altar, and over them was
spread a pall of fair white silk, with tapers burning round,
and richly emblazoned banners waving over.   Thus
lying in state, it awaited the erection of a costly monu-
ment, till St. Hugh commanded its expulsion.   But the
nuns remembered their poor sister, whom they had laid

to rest in that open grave; and when the bishop died,
they gathered her bones from out the place of their in-
terment into a bag, which they inclosed in a leather
case, and tenderly deposited before the altar.

The altar has long since been broken, and the place
wherein the memorial tent, with its pall of fair white
silk, was stationed, is roofless now. Instead of tapers
burning round, and emblazoned banners waving over,
springs up a solitary nut-tree—the Nut-tree of Rosa-
mond's grave. It bears a profusion of nuts, but without
kernels, empty as the deceptive pleasures of this world's
pageants.*

And silent too, sad, vacant, and unpeopled, is the
mound on which once stood the castle of William
Longespé, poor Rosamond's eldest son. It was a drear
and treeless elevation, rising over the wide extent of
downs, that were seen spreading far as the eye could
reach; yet there were glad hearts within, young children
and cheerful voices, the lady Ela and William Longespé,
with their visitors and dependants, and those who came
and went, making that stately castle to seem a royal
residence.

William Longespé was distinguished for his chivalry
and feats of arms, the lady Ela for her mild and benig-
nant virtues. They had married in early life, and her
estates and honours, according to the customs of the
feudal ages, had served to enoble a brave and deserving

* Southey's visit to Godstow nunnery.—CAMDEN.

youth, who had no other patrimony than his sword.
Ela was born among the beautiful shades of Amesbury,
whither her mother had retired before her birth.   It was
called the ladies' bower, and was appended to the castle
of Salisbury, as that of Woodstock to Oxford castle,
and there her young days passed among trees and
flowers, till, as years passed on, she became the delight
and ornament of her father's court.   Earl William stood
high in favour with King Richard.   He carried the
dove-surmounted verge, or rod, before that monarch at
his coronation; and to him was confided the responsible
office of keeping the king's charter, for licensing
tournaments throughout the country.*   His titular
castle frowned over the stern ramparts of Sarisbyrig,
where no stream was heard to murmur, nor the
song of birds came remotely on the ear, except the
joyous warble of the soaring lark, or the simple un-
varied note of the whinchat, seeking its insect food
among the thyme hills.   But instead of woods and
streams, the castle was surrounded with extensive downs,
covered with short herbage, and in the space where
two valleys obliquely intersected each other, was one
of the five fields, or steads, for the holding of feats of
arms.   The field was full in view of the majestic fortress
of old Sarum, and although it seemed as a dip, or rather
hollow in the elevated downs, it afforded ample space
for the combatants and spectators, and those who stood

* Roger de Hoveden.

on the highest point of what—had seats been cut in the
broad slope—might have been termed an amphitheatre,
looked down on the rich and smiling banks of the Avon
and the Nadder, with the venerable towers of Wilton
Abbey.*   Here then, were often witnessed the proudest
exhibitions of chivalric enterprise, and often did the
little Ela gaze with awe and wonder from the windows
of her father's castle, on knight and banners, and all the
pomp and pageantry of those heroic games.

Scarcely, however, had Ela attained her eighth year,
when the Earl of Salisbury having died, after a short ill-
ness, she became the orphan heiress of his princely patri-
mony, and an exile; for scarcely had the banners, and
the scutcheons, and the mutes passed by, and all the
pomp of death went after him to his last resting-place,
than the little Ela suddenly disappeared, and was
nowhere to be found.   Some said that her mother
sought her sorrowing; others, that she gave but little
heed, and that while knights and servants rode the
country over, asking questions of all they met, and
exploring every brake and hollow on the ample downs;
returning ever and anon, either with some hope of
finding the lost child, or else to consult with her lady
mother concerning the next course to pursue; she alone
seemed as if indifferent to the matter.   The countess
had large possessions in Normandy or Champaign, and
it was at length conjectured that the orphan had been

* Hatcher's Account of Salisbury.

sent to her relations, lest King Richard should avail himself of his feudal right, to marry her according to his will.   But such was not the case, though true in part, as respected her distant home.   Ela had three uncles, of whom the eldest was next heir to the great possessions of the deceased earl.   No historic light gleams on the biography of these kinsmen, excepting that being younger brothers, without patrimony, and unmarried, they retired into the monastery of Bradenstoke.*   Yet tradition tells, that when the elder brother heard of Ela's fatherless condition, he threw aside his cowl, and assumed the cuirass.   It might have been, that often in the silence and the solitude of that old abbey, when passing its dimly-lighted cloisters, dark thoughts had worked within him; that scowling on his books and beads, he had contrasted his condition as a poor and obscure monk, with the grandeur and the vast possessions of the earldom of Salisbury. The pope absolved him from vows of poverty, for thus it is recorded in the traditions of the place, and forth he came, a claimant to the honours and the wealth of that illustrious house.   Tradition lingers among old walls and deserted hearths; there may be nothing for history to glean, but her lowlier sister loves to keep alive the feeble glimmering of her lone lamp, in places from whence all other light is gone.

Rightly, therefore, did the anxious and affectionate

* The Old Peerage, by Brooke.

F

mother of young Ela seek to remove her daughter from
the reach of one whose ambitious and turbulent dispo-
sition might have prompted him to crime. But the
days in which she lived were those of stirring incidents.
A train of gallant troubadours gave life and animation to
the court of lion-hearted Richard, and the mysterious
disappearance of the orphan heiress was with them a
theme of frequent conjecture and resolve. An English
knight, of the name of William Talbot, inspired, it
would seem, by the romantic adventures of the min-
strel Blondel, resolved to find out the place of her con-
cealment. He went forth attired as a pilgrim, with his
staff and cockle-shell, and having landed on the coast of
Normandy, he wandered to and fro, for the space of two
years,* as if in quest of the shrine at which he sought
to pay his vows. There were shrines in the depth of
solitary forests, and to such he bent his way, others in
populous towns, and before them he would duly kneel,
asking questions of those he met, and warily seeking to
discover where the lost one was concealed. At length,
so the poet tells, he saw a maiden, whose English
accent and fair hair denoted her foreign birth, come
forth with her companions from a castle on the coast.
Talbot concealed himself behind a rock, and listened
while the maiden, who was gathering shells from off
the sand, spoke of the far country whence she came.

* Dugdale incorrectly says months, instead of years, a mistake
corrected by Bowles.

It seemed to him that she gazed wistfully over the wide sea, and when the dew began to fall, and the bell tolled out from the grey turret, she looked back from beneath the postern, as if to catch a last glimpse of the dim waters. Laying aside his pilgrim dress, he assumed that of a wandering troubadour, and gained admittance to the inmates of the castle. He recounted the deeds of former times, concerning the perils of King Richard, and how the minstrel Blondel, wandering through storm and sunshine, had found the prison of his master. He repeated the wild strain which Blondel had sung before the old fortress, and the answering melody that responded from within; and thus in sentiment, if not in words, for the thoughts are those of the minstrel Peter d'Auvergne, the gallant Talbot made known his errand to the orphan daughter.*

> Haste, haste thee, haste, my faithful bird,
>   O'er the tumbling and tossing sea,
> Breathe to my love the sighs you have heard,
>   And her answer respond to me.
>
> O, the fond bird flew from the green hill's side,
>   Where blossoming roses blow,
> She spread her wing o'er the ocean wide,
>   While the blue waves danced below.
>
> And the strains which she sang to the evening star,
>   As it rose o'er the darkling hill,
> She pour'd forth again to the lov'd one afar,
>   By the gush of the flowing rill.

* History of Lacock Abbey. Monsieur de Saint Palage's great work on the History of Troubadours.

The lady heard in her lonely bower,
  As she gazed on the wandering moon;
When her pale beams brightened the old grey tower,
  Riding now in her highest noon.

Ah! thou dost not heed my plaintive strain,
  For thus the fair bird sang;
I have flown in my haste o'er the stormy main,
  From groves where my music rang.

Where my music rang, when the glow-worm's light
  Glimmer'd oft in the darkling glen,
And no sounds were heard 'mid the stilly night,
  From the homes, or the haunts of men.

Save from one, who fear'd not the dew nor the damp,
  Who told me his true love tale,
As he linger'd alone, by the glow-worm's lamp,
  In the depth of the hawthorn dale.

Methinks e'en now, o'er the dewy grass,
  All alone on the moonlit plain,
Will his constant step, 'mid the dim light pass,
  To list for my answering strain.

And that answering strain the young knight heard,
  As he stole from his castle hall,
For the lady breathed low to the faithful bird,
  Words of love from her distant thrall.

Thus sung the troubadour, and the maiden longed to see again the wide downs on which her young eyes had gazed, for she knew not the thraldom that awaited a rich heiress in those days of feudal tyranny. The book of Lacock is silent with regard to the means by which the troubadour contrived to bear her off, concerning her perils by sea or land, or her joyous meeting with her widowed

mother. The book tells merely, that King Richard bestowed
her hand on his brother Longespé, and with it the vast pos-
sessions and the title of the Earl of Salisbury. Longespé was
then a youth, just rising into manhood,* and happy was
it for the orphan heiress that King Richard gave her to
one whom she could love.   For it happened not unfre-
quently that great heiresses were married to stern men,
either that their lands might enrich the younger sons of
royalty, or else to repay services that had been rendered
the crown.   It is generally conjectured, that Richard
designed the Lady Ela for his brother from the period of his
father's death, when the hostile conduct of her uncle
occasioned the young child to be sent away.   His faith-
ful Talbot sought and found her, most probably by the
desire of the king, for he was loyal and experienced, and
in none of the minstrel knights whom he admitted as
companions to the festive board, did King Richard more
unreservedly confide.   He was proud, also, to be num-
bered among the devoted friends of the youthful
Longespé, and in after years his name occurs among
the witnesses to several charters given by the earl.†
Whether, therefore, he was a friend of Longespé from
his days of boyhood, or whether he had earned that
friendship by his services in recovering the lovely Ela, cer-
tain it is, that neither his friendship nor his services were
forgotten, and that when Longespé obtained the honours

* Book of Lacock.
† Close Rolls, May 2. Rhymer's Fœdore, 1207.

and possessions of the house of Salisbury, Talbot became an inmate of his castle.*

Ela returned to her father's hall, to the old castle of Sarum, from which she had looked in her childhood on the feats of arms that were exhibited in the tournament arena. But those days had passed, for King John, who now filled the throne, cared little for jousts or minstrelsy. His thoughts brooded in sullen mood on the discontents that were abroad, and on the distracted condition of the country. Meanwhile the chivalrous and devoted Longespé accompanied King John, who went from place to place like the wild Arab, staying nowhere, ever restless and inconstant. The Lady Ela occasionally accompanied her husband in his expeditions, but she preferred the order and dignity of her own well-regulated household to the migrations of the court. The earl, too, was often weary of his mode of life, but his affection to his brother made him willing to relinquish his home comforts, and if the king was ever sincerely attached to any human being, it was to the gallant Longespé. There is little doubt but that his affection for the earl induced him to erect a tomb to the memory of his unhappy mother, whose remains had been removed from the place of their interment; it was tastefully embossed with fine brass, and had an inscription around the edge.†

* Book of Lacock.

† A most beautiful copy was deposited, and may still be seen, in the chamber of Records at Salisbury Cathedral.

When the differences that existed between the monarch
and his barons arose to a fearful height, and the month
of June witnessed the proud triumph of the rebel chiefs,
and the acquisition of Magna Charta, on the field
of Runnimede, the brother stood unshaken in his fidelity.
Many had transferred their allegiance from the king to
the prevailing party, and John was reduced by an im-
perious necessity to a reluctant and insincere concession;
but the banners of the Earl of Salisbury* floated in the
camp of his royal kinsman, together with those of the
Earls of Pembroke, Arundel, and Warren.   The country
was quiet for a season, but at length disturbances broke
out again.   It was no longer safe to venture unattended,
by an armed force, beyond the precincts of the castle,
and the "most dear friend and brother" of the wayward
monarch, shared in the disasters of his reign.   At one
time a prisoner,† at another deputed to place garrisons
in the castles of Windsor, Hertford, and Berkhampstead,
and to cut off supplies from the city of London, where the
insurgents had fixed themselves.   At length, hardened
by the scenes of misery to which he had been accus-
tomed, his kindlier feelings seemed to be totally ob-
scured.   Marching at the head of troops, with the fierce
Falcasius de Breant, the earl imbibed his spirit, and
shared in his enormities.   Before them was often a smil-
ing and well-peopled country, behind them a desolate

* Clause Rolls.

† Dugdale, from a MS. Oxon, in Bibl. Bodl. n. 11. f. 177, et 178. p. a.

wilderness,* and while the earl and Falcasius were thus
mercilessly occupied, the king's arms spread equal deso-
lation in other parts, till at length the castles of Mount-
sorrel, in Leicestershire, and that of Robert de Ros, in
Yorkshire, alone remained to the insurgent barons.   To
this succeeded the coming over of the French king, in
order to assist the barons, the seeming defection of the
earl, the death of John, and the coronation of young
Henry.   The country was again at peace, and Longespé
returned to his home and family.   With the passing
away of battle scenes, seemed to have passed also the
fierce spirit of the earl.   We hear of him as a kind hus-
band and indulgent father, as a bounteous master, and
one who loved to promote good works.   The gentle
influence of Lady Ela apparently recalled him to the mood
of better days, as the associating with De Breant had
urged him to deeds of rapine and injustice.   The beau-
tiful cathedral of Salisbury was founded by him, and
thither came, at his request, the bishop of the diocese,
with a few earls and barons, and a vast concourse of
people from all parts, on the day appointed for laying
the first stone.   Divine service having been performed in
the ancient edifice, the bishop put off his shoes, and
walked in procession with his clergy to the site of the
new foundation, singing the litany as they went.   The
bishop then addressed the people, and taking a stone in
his hand, he placed it in the name of Pope Honorius,

* Matt. of Paris.   Clause Rolls.

and afterwards another, for the Archbishop of Canterbury. The fourth was laid by the Earl of Salisbury, the fifth by the Countess Ela, "a truly praise-worthy woman," as wrote William de Wanda, afterwards Dean of Sarum, "because she was filled with the fear of the Lord." Other stones were added by a few noblemen, archdeacons, and canons of the church of Sarum, amidst the acclamations of the assembled multitude, many of whom wept for joy, and gladly contributed according to their ability. A negociation was then pending with the Welch at Tewkesbury, or the company would have been much larger, but most of the nobility who passed that way on their return, requested leave to add each a stone, and some bound themselves to make contributions for the next seven years.*

To this succeeded the stern and stirring incidents of war, for King Henry's brother, having recently received the honour of knighthood, with the earldoms of Cornwall and Poictou, it was resolved that he should commence his military career on the plains of Gascony, under the guidance of his uncle, the Earl of Salisbury, and Philip de Albeney.† Forth, then, they went, with sixty knights and their attendants, and an army of French and English, and again were homes despoiled, and castles set on fire, and fields and vineyards trodden down by hostile

---

* Register of Osmund, among the MSS. of the Cathedral. Narrative, by William de Wanda, published in the first volume of Wilkins's Concilia.

† Matt. Paris. Fœdera.

steps, till, having achieved the purpose of their preda-
tory warfare, the earl and his companions embarked
for England. But the nights were dark, and October
winds, gathering strength and fierceness from the early
setting in of a long winter, tost their unwieldy ships like
cockle-shells on the face of the deep waters. The chief-
tains despaired of life, as did the bravest of the seamen,
and the earl resolved to throw overboard whatever he
possessed, either of rings, or gold, or silver, rich vest-
ments, or scutcheoned banners, that as he had entered
life unprovided with them, so he might pass in like
manner to his eternal home. But a waxen light, of large
size and brilliancy, was seen by all on board, suddenly
appearing on the summit of the mast, and near it stood a
female of surpassing beauty, who preserved that warning
light, shining in the midnight darkness, from being
extinguished by the wind or rain. Seeing this, the
mariners took courage, and when the day began
to dawn, the violence of the storm abated, a fresh
gale sprung up, and urged the ship onward to the
isle of Rhé, about three miles distant from Rochelle.
As they neared the coast, an old abbey came in sight, and
thither the earl sent messengers on landing, requesting
favour and protection, and that he might remain concealed
from his enemies till a fair wind should admit of his
returning home. To this the abbot gave consent, and
received both the earl and his companions with kindness
and hospitality. But the island was in charge of Savaric

de Maloleone, who served the French king, and kept
watch over the adjoining coast, and great peril would
have accrued to Earl William, had not two of Maloleone's
retainers gone secretly to the abbey and warned him to
remain no longer, telling him, that unless he left the
island before the following morning, he would be cap-
tured by their comrades, who guarded the island and the
straits.   Upon this the earl, after presenting them with
twenty pounds sterling, hastened to the shore, from which
the whole company embarked on a raging sea.   They
trusted, as the distance was but short, that they should
speedily gain the English coast, but in this they were
mistaken, and, for three long wintry months, did those
ill-fated men struggle with the raging elements, before
they arrived within sight of land.*

Meanwhile, the Lady Ela hoped from day to day that
the earl might yet return, but, still as weeks past on, and
the storms of winter gathered strength, she began to fear
that his ships had been lost at sea.   There were also
other wives and mothers, who suffered as intensely as the
countess, for among the knights and soldiers that accom-
panied him on his perilous undertaking, many had
families at home, who looked wistfully for their return.
But the Lady Ela had trials that especially attended her
high rank and large possessions, for although a matron,
whose age and dignity might have commanded more
respect, she became an object of pursuit to the fortune-

* Matt. Paris.

hunters of the court. Hubert de Burgh, who stood high
in favour with Henry III., sought for his nephew the
hand of the widowed countess, and the youth, entering
with a kindred spirit into the interested views of his
ambitious kinsman, prepared for the undertaking. De
Burgh had been twice at Salisbury in attendance on
the king during the earl's perilous voyage,* and
it is therefore not surprising that the future disposal
of the honours and broad lands of the Lady Ela should
have become an object of his speculations. Henry
III. was said to be much afflicted by the supposed death
of the earl, but when De Burgh petitioned that he would
permit his inheritance to pass with the Lady Ela into
his own family, the king readily gave leave, on condition
that the countess could be induced to consent. The
justiciary, for such was the office of De Burgh, accordingly
dispatched his nephew, on a courser richly caparisoned,
with knights and squires sumptuously arrayed, that he
might present himself in a distinguished manner before the
countess. But the lady scorned his suit; she heeded
neither his flattering speeches nor large promises, and
she told him, with becoming dignity, that messengers
had arrived from her absent husband, bringing the wel-
come news that he was both safe and well. She added,
further, that if indeed the earl was dead, she would in
no wise receive the nephew of the Justiciary De Burgh as
a second husband. " Therefore," said she, " you may

* William de Wanda's Church History.

seek a marriage elsewhere, because you find that you
have come hither in vain." On hearing this, Reimund
de Burgh became exceedingly crest-fallen, and, having
remounted his gaily trapped courser, he hurried from the
castle with his train.*

The earl returned to his home on the fourth of the
ides of January, and went the following day to see the
king, who was then ill at Marlborough. He made a
heavy complaint to his royal nephew, that base men had
been allowed to insult his countess with proffers unworthy
of her. He had been abroad, he said, and suffered much
in the king's service, and it seemed hard that advantage
should be taken of his protracted absence by the Justi-
ciary de Burgh, to send a certain low-bred man, who was
not even a knight, into the presence of his wife, with the
intention of constraining her to an unlawful marriage, had
she not most nobly repelled him. He added, moreover,
that unless the king caused full reparation to be made by
the justiciary, for so great an outrage, he would himself seek
redress, though it should involve a serious disturbance of
the country. The king, who was greatly rejoiced to see his
uncle, well knowing that he was both powerful and valor-
ous, did not attempt to excuse himself, and the Justiciary
de Burg being present at the interview, wisely resolved
to atone for his misconduct, by confessing that the fault
rested with him. He besought the earl to pass the mat-
ter over, and to accept, as a proof of his forgiveness,

* History of Lacock.   Matt. Paris.

some fine horses, and other costly gifts.   He next
invited the earl to dine with him, who went accordingly
on the day appointed, but being taken ill immediately
after dinner, he was obliged to return home.   Rumours
went abroad that poison had been administered, but the
character of De Burgh does not warrant any suspicion of
the kind.*   The hardships which the earl sustained
while abroad, with his subsequent agitation, occasioned by
the insult offered to his countess, were sufficient to account
for his sudden illness.   Finding himself dying, he sent
for the Bishop of Salisbury, that he might receive in the
confession and viaticum, such blessings as were needful
to one in his condition.   The bishop came immediately,
and, when he entered the apartment, bearing with him
the sacred elements, the earl sprung from his bed, and
hastily tying a rough noose about his neck, he threw him-
self weeping upon the floor.   He was, he said, a traitor
to the Most High, and could not rise till he had con-
fessed his past sins, and received the communion of the
life-giving sacrament, that he might testify himself to be
the servant of his Creator.   He afterwards continued for
some days in prayer, and such acts of penitence as his
faith enjoined, and he then peaceably yielded up his
soul to his Redeemer; † to Him "who willeth not the
death of a sinner, but rather that he should turn from his
wickedness and live."

The earl died on the seventh of March, 1226, and

* History of Lacock Abbey.   † Matt. of Westminster.

his corpse, according to the fashion of the age, was immediately removed to the cathedral of New Sarum. The day was stormy, and loud gusts of wind, accompanied with heavy rain, swept over the open downs, but still the funeral train went on, with its long, long line of torches, for it might not be that the corpse of one who had been so great on earth, should remain from out the sacred walls of the cathedral which he had founded. It was about a mile from the castle to the church, and a multitude of people followed; some were loud in their lamentations, others wept silently as they went; for the earl had been a kind master, and it seemed hard that he should so soon be taken from them, who had but just returned to his home. They remembered, too, that only eight weeks before, and at the same hour of the day, he had passed through the wide portals of the magnificent cathedral to offer praises and thanksgivings for his preservation and safe return; that on the very spot where he was then received in procession by the clergy, with great demonstrations of joy,* the same company was coming forth to meet him, who was now being borne a corpse before them; for the bier was met at the western door by the bishop and the neighbouring chieftains, with the cathedral clergy, choristers, and precentor, chanting in Latin as they passed up the nave, the same funeral service which is now chanted in English, on occasions of public funerals within the walls of cathedrals.

* Chron. of W. de Wanda.   Wilkin's Concilia, vol. I page 559.

His martial figure of grey marble still reposes on his tomb, sleeping, as it were, from century to century with his sword and shield. The features of this son, and brother, and uncle of kings, are only partially exposed, through a small aperture in the hood of mail, which covers his mouth and chin, the eyebrows betoken some-what of a lofty and impetuous feeling, but the eyes seem gentle and intelligent.*

The day of death is light, in comparison of its bitter-ness, with that of the interment. In the former case, the spirit indeed has passed away, yet the form remains. The wife, or child, or parent can sit beside the couch, and gaze on the still unchanged features. But when the grave has once closed upon the loved one, what words can tell the utter desolation that presses on the heart ! Thus felt the Lady Ela, when the last words of the solemn service ceased, when the sound of footsteps neared to the grave's edge, and somewhat heavy seemed to be letting down into the darkness and the depth,—when her half-averted eye looked for the last time on the narrow coffin, resting now within the grave, but soon to be concealed for ever. Lady Ela heeded not the words of comfort which the pale priest spoke, nor yet the solemn chanting that burst forth again, as if to bear her spirit up with holy hopes from out the wretchedness of her sad lot. But the Lord, in whom she trusted, did not forsake her, and when she returned to her home,

* Annals and Antiquities of Lacock Abbey.

it was with a firm resolve to devote herself to the service of her Maker, by cherishing the memory of her husband, and taking care of her large family.

It was happy for the Lady Ela that she was suffered to remain in free widowhood; that even the powerful Justiciary de Burgh and his aspiring nephew dared not molest her. This was an especial favour, and as such the countess ever regarded it, for ladies of large estates were rarely permitted to continue single; their lands and dignities passed by right of inheritance to persons whom they were often constrained to marry.* Thus, at the same period of English history, the rich heiress of Albemarle conferred the title of earl successively on her three husbands, William Mandeville, William de Fortibus, and Baldwin de Betun. The countess, therefore, being priviliged to continue in a widowed state, exercised the office of Sheriff of Wiltshire, and that of Castellan of Old Sarum, even when her son became of age, and claimed, by his mother's wish, the investiture of the earldom; the king his cousin refused it, not in displeasure, but according to the principles of feudal law; and hence it happened, that in consequence of the Lady Ela's protracted life, the earldom of Salisbury continued dormant, and as she survived both her son and grandson, it was never renewed in the house of Longespé. The great seal with which the countess ratified the many legal instruments that were required in the administra-

* Book of Lacock Abbey.

tion of her feudal rights is still extant. We may not
perhaps regard it as presenting a portrait of the Countess
Ela, like the effigy of her husband in Salisbury cathe-
dral, but it affords, no doubt, a faithful resemblance of
her noble and dignified bearing, and of her graceful,
though simple costume. Her right hand is on her
breast, her left supports a hawk, the usual symbol of
nobility, her head is covered with a singularly small cap,
possibly, the precursor of the more recent coronet; her
long hair flows negligently upon her neck, and on either
side the royal lions of Salisbury appear to gaze on her,
like the lions of Spenser's " Fairy Queen," on the deso-
late lady Una.*

Seven years had now elapsed from the time of the
earl's death, during which the countess sedulously ful-
filled the duties of her high condition. Her eldest son,
who was then a minor, married the rich heiress of two
baronies, the daughter of Richard de Camville, and the
Lady Eustachia.† Richard, Stephen, and Nicholas
were gone forth into the world, and her daughters
Isabella, Petronilla, Ela, and Sola being either married
or of age, the countess thought herself at liberty to
relinquish the arduous duties in which she had hitherto
been engaged, and to devote herself to a secluded life.
Yielding, therefore, to the natural desire of withdrawing
from the busy world, she proceeded to undertake a task

* Annals of Lacock, p. 180.
† Madox's History of the Exchequer, p. 218.

that was calculated as much for a season to add to her
employments, as it afterwards contributed to her repose.

River scenery has ever been a passion with me. I
can gaze unwearied on the tranquil flowing of deep, clear
waters, now shaded with old trees, that droop their
branches to the water's edge, and now by rock and
underwood, where roses and wild honeysuckles, harebells,
and primroses mingle their beauty and their fragrance.
Such is the tranquil Avon, passing in gloom and depth,
dark, silent, and unruffled, among rocks and trees ; or
murmuring in its onward course, with that calm sound of
moving waters which seems to tell of peace and solitude. It
is flowing now, through a spacious and level meadow, with
tall elms, and cattle feeding on its margin, and in the
distance, high spiral chimneys appear at intervals among
the trees.   They belong to the ancient nunnery of
Lacock, which the Lady Ela founded ; not standing as
many stand, with smokeless chimneys, lone and tenant-
less, over which the creeping ivy and wild wall-flower
seek to hide the rents of ruin, but dwelt in still ; a
place where the living may think of those who are resting
in the cells beneath, who have neither heard the winds
of winter, nor felt the cheering sunbeams for more than
six hundred years.

This spacious and level meadow, with its tall elms and
cattle, was once a glade ; this bright river, now journey-
ing in shade and sunshine along peopled districts, flowed
once in silence and in loneliness through the ancient

forests of Chippenham and Melksham. Yonder, and at a
distance over the wide wood, rises the high and lonely
arch of Malmesbury Abbey, the "august, but melancholy
mother," as the poet Bowles has well observed, with a
poet's feeling, of many a cell or monastery beside the
Avon.   Battlements and buttresses, seen far off in the
bright sunshine, point out the remains of Bradenstoke
Abbey, rising among old trees, and seeming to overlook
the river as it winds through the vale and pastures of
Somerford and Christian Malford.   Scarcely a vestige
remains of Stanley priory; its walls are low and roofless,
but the bright blue "forget-me-not," nestling itself
among ferns and foxgloves in the fissures of the walls,
seems to call upon the passenger to remember that men
once thought, and felt, and suffered, where all now is
silent and deserted—an emblem-flower, a living motto,
inscribed on the wrecks of ruin.   But Lacock Abbey,
standing on the verge of the spacious and level meadow,
is still inhabited, and its cloisters are fresh, as if they
were just completed, although the arches are hung with
ivy.   More than six centuries have passed since the
Countess of Salisbury came, in the year 1232, accom-
panied by such persons as she loved to consort with, to
this remote part of her hereditary domain.   The woods
around were bursting into leaf, and the "one word
spoken" of the contented cuckoo was heard at intervals.

It was early in the month of April,* and as yet the

* Book of Lacock.

winds were chill, but April was in unison with her past life, one of storm and sunshine, and now about to close, as respected this world's turmoils, amid the beautiful scenes of woodland and of river.   Two monasteries were founded by the countess on that memorable day ; Lacock, which she designed for her own abode, in which holy canonesses might dwell, continually and devoutly serving the Most High ; the other, the priory of Henton, of the Carthusian order.*   It was believed that the countess in thus founding these religious establishments, desired to perform the vows of her husband, which he made during his great perils, when returning from Gascony to England.   A few years more, and the bright sun which beamed on the day of the foundation of Lacock nunnery, looked down on a dark marble stone, which men placed, with heavy hearts, over the remains of its noble foundress. " As I stood, in a moody day of the declining year," wrote one,† who has recorded with deep feeling the long-forgotten history of the Lady Ela, "and thought of her youthful romantic history, a gleam of pale sunshine struggled through the dark drapery of ivy, and fell upon the spot. At the same moment a wintry bird, which had taken shelter among the branches, piped one small note ; no other sound was heard amid the profound silence of the place, and as the short note ceased, the gleam faded also."

* Book of Lacock.   † Historian of Lacock Abbey.

Dunmow Priory.

Dunmow Priory.

The old tree, the old tree,
   Has fallen long ago;
But I shall tell of thee, old tree,
   As if thou wert standing now.

How thy ample branches spread,
   In the days of ruthless John ;
How they waved o'er the silent dead,
   When the last dread deed was done.—M. R.

DANCING lights and shadows are playing on the tomb of
Lady Marian.* They are cast by the old tree whose
waving branches, seen through the lofty window, with its
tracery and mullions, grey and time-worn, recall to my
mind the day in which it stood with its brotherhood
beside the little church of Dunmow, when bold Robin-
hood, the outlawed Earl of Huntingdon, passed and
repassed with his lady and their archers through the
green recesses of Sherwood forest. The contiguous
priory was standing then, but this memorial of the olden
time, the present church of Dunmow, formed merely the
south aisle of a magnificent collegiate church, and of a

* Marian is the legendary name of the Countess of Huntingdon.

religious house founded many years before the days of
Robinhood, by the sister of Raef Baynard, who held the
manor in the time of Domesday survey.　Far and near
extended a wild forest with its glens and dingles, but farm-
houses are standing now where the wolf used to range,
and a public road passes within sight of the ancient
building, from which it is divided by a corn-field, and
burying-ground, with head-stones worn and lichen-dotted,
and crumbling from long exposure to the weather.　How
still and solemn is this place !　Here knees have bent in
prayer for successive generations, and here successive
generations have been laid to rest ; the poor beside the
church—a few of noble birth within the walls.　Sir
Walter Bohun is one of these.　His plate armour and
leathern shirt indicate that his days were passed in warlike
deeds, and beside him rests his lady, dame Matilda, who
wears the insignia of her courtly rank ; her tiara and lace, her
earrings and her necklace. Their heads repose on cushions,
and their hands are raised in the attitude of prayer.　The
effigies of both have suffered ; the legs of Sir Walter are
broken at the knees, and the delicate fret-work of the
lace which adorns his lady has been rudely handled.
Other steps than those which used to tread softly, as
befits a house of prayer, were heard here when this
deed was done.　Men, with peaked beards and round
hats, halted beneath the Oak of Dunmow, and they
thought they did good service to their Maker when they
despoiled the old effigies ; they, too, have passed from

among the living, and though their sojourn occasioned
great distress and terror in the neighbourhood, no trace of
them remains at Dunmow, excepting in the mischief
which they did.　Sir James Hallet rests here also, and a
few mural monuments remain upon the walls, but the
one tomb, which of all others is most dear, upon which
the quivering lights and shadows play, and sunbeams
shed a softened radiance, is that of the Lady Marian.
Shielded by a beautiful screen of dark old oak, coeval
with the building, and which separates the nave from
the chancel ; it stands forth in bold relief, a relic of
the olden time, which the convulsions of ages—foreign
wars and civil feuds, have yet spared.　The head is
covered with a woollen coif, the neck encircled with a
collar, and a string of pendants falls upon an embroidered
cape; a rich girdle and long robe, with sleeves close to
the wrists, and hands covered with rings further indicate
her rank.　Angels were stationed beside the head, and a
dog crouched on either side her feet.　But rough hands
marred this tomb also, the angels, who seemed to watch
over the sleeping effigy, were rudely broken, though the
effigy itself was spared.　Perhaps the lady who lay within
the tomb was associated with the fondest recollections of
the rebel leader.　It may be, that he had gathered nuts amid
the open spaces of the forest where she dwelt ; before
years of crime and peril had hardened his young
heart, or, perhaps, when sick and restless upon his bed,
his mother might have told him concerning the Lady

G

Marian's woes and wanderings; how she fled from her
father's castle, when that castle was in flames, and how
bold Robinhood and Little John shielded her from harm.

More than six hundred years have passed away since
a company of monks from the adjacent priory brought
hither the corpse of Lady Marian to inter it within the
church; since the boughs of the old tree, waving in the
cold night air, cast their uncertain shadows on the long
train of veiled nuns, as they entered by torch-light the
low arched door-way of the church.

Marian had passed her young days in Baynard castle,
on the borders of Sherwood Forest.   Her father, Richard
Fitz Walter, gave a tournament when his daughter attained
her eighteenth year; knights and squires assembled
from all parts; ladies came attired in robes of costly silk;
and during three whole days, jousts and sports continued
without intermission; but on the fourth, a stranger, clad
in burnished mail, entered the lists and vanquished the
bravest of his competitors.   No one knew whence he
came, but his gallant bearing and handsome countenance,
won the heart of the young queen of that high festival,
and she trembled when she hung the golden chain around
his neck.   It was said, too, by those who looked on, that
the mysterious victor was observed to turn pale; but he
departed as he entered, suddenly and in haste, and the
tramp of his stately steed was heard afar in the still forest.

Prince John was at the banquet, yet he liked not the
noble owner of the castle; he had no thoughts in common

with those of a true and loyal knight, and having been
reproved for some evil expressions he went away in anger,
and vowed revenge. A few short months and the brother of
Fitz Walter departed for the Holy Land, taking with him
a considerable number of his brother's men-at-arms, when
John, watching his opportunity, led on an armed band
against the castle, and slew its owner. Marian fled to
the green forest, where she wandered all the day,
and concealed herself at night among the underwood.
The next day, she met the stranger knight, whom
she had crowned a short time before, when Baynard
castle was in all its pride, and her father presided there.
His burnished coat of mail was laid aside, and a simple
suit of Lincoln green betokened his mode of life. Soothly
did he greet the lady, and told her not to fear, for though
he was Robinhood, the outlawed Earl of Huntingdon,
at the mention of whose name stern warriors trembled
in their halls, and ecclesiastics turned pale, his good
men should shield her well.

Lady Marian laid aside her whimple and her veil, and
the better to conceal herself, put on a light kind of
armour, such as young men wore on days of festival, for
she had not strength to bear the heavy casque and buck-
ler. In this garb she encountered King John, who
called upon her to surrender; but he who stood before
her was the murderer of her father, and what will not the
recollection of such a deed produce in even the gentlest
bosom; in one, too, who, perhaps, had not been taught the

blessed precept which teaches to forgive. "Yield," said the prince, for he knew not the damsel in her strange attire; he thought, most probably, that the youth before him was in the service of the outlaw, and that his command would be sufficient to enforce obedience. The stranger was not thus to be subdued, and so firmly did she maintain her assumed character, that the prince was obliged to with-draw. John heard that his antagonist was no other than the young flower of Baynard castle, Marian, whose father he had slain, and he resolved to be avenged on her also.

Maid Marian became the wife of Robinhood, and when King Richard restored to him his earldom and estates, she presided in his baronial hall with equal courtesy and magnificence. John succeeded to the throne on his brother's death, and then the vengeance which had long brooded in his sullen breast fell heavy on the earl; he was again outlawed, and for many long and weary years did his fair young wife follow his fortunes. Time, and the hardships which he endured, had at length weakened the strength of the bold outlaw. He tried his shafts one morning, and finding that they neither flew so far, nor so fast as his strong arm was wont to send them, he resolved to repair to Kirkley nunnery, where his cousin presided as prioress. He had heard much of her skill in medicine, and hoped that she might stay the fever that raged in his veins. "Thrice welcome, cousin Robert," she said, but treachery was in her heart, for she bore no good-will to him who plundered both the church and churchmen. Robert passed through the strong oaken door, but he returned not again, save as a corpse borne by his tall bowmen wearily along, to bury beneath some fine trees near Kirkley.

At this sad period of her life the countess took refuge in Dunmow Priory. It stood in a wild and secluded spot on the borders of Sherwood Forest; that great forest to which she had fled for refuge in her young days, and where her married life had passed. John heard that she was there, and he rejoiced in the thought of vengeance, for he remembered their rencounter in years gone by, and how she had worsted him on that memorable day. Summoning, therefore, a gallant knight, Robert de Medeive, common ancestor of the present Earl Manvers, and of one, to whom we owe this biographic memoranda of the Lady Marian, he bade him go with all speed to the Priory of Dunmow, and present to the Countess of Huntingdon a valuable bracelet, as a token of amity and reconciliation. Years chequered with much of sorrow had passed since the fall of Baynard castle; since the encounter of Marian and the prince in Sherwood Forest; perhaps she had learned in her cell, the blessedness and the duty of forgiveness. Walter had heard concerning the noble lady who thus cordially received him as an herald from the king—of the sufferings of her young days, and how the brave Earl Huntingdon had given her a home when her own fair patrimony was in the hands of strangers. Her bloom, indeed, had faded, together with the sprightliness which rendered her the darling of her father's house; but her noble bearing and matron beauty which time still spared, caused the rough warrior to gaze on her with mingled love and admiration. But he wished not to be thus entangled, and, therefore, bidding her adieu, he hastened on his way. The way was long and lonely, now over a wide common; now through the depth of a dark forest, beside a rapid streamlet, or through a valley where high trees drooped on either side, in all the majesty and luxuriance of uncultivated nature. The knight looked not on these, however beautiful; he cared not for the grandeur or sublimity of the mighty landscape, which extended at times before him, or the sylvan beauty of woodland scenery; he thought only of the high-minded dame to whom he had borne the pledge of amity; till at length her image rose before him with an intensity of feeling that caused him to turn his horse's head, and to retrace the way which he had come. The day had closed in before he reached the priory, but the light of many tapers streamed through the windows of the adjoining church on the weary knight, and the dirge of death sounded solemnly through the stillness of the forest. The priory seemed deserted; there was no one to answer his impatient questions; all were either within the church or around the door, and thither he too hastened with trembling steps, for his heart sunk within him. The chancel was lighted up, and before the curiously carved

screen of dark old oak lay the corpse of the Lady Marian;
it was covered with flowers according to the fashion of
the age, for as yet this custom of the olden time was not
laid aside. The bracelet was on her wrist; its fiery
poison had dried her life's blood, and cankered the flesh
it touched. Her face was ghastly pale, but a heavenly
smile irradiated her fine countenance; it told that all
within was peace—that even the last dire deed had not
disturbed her thought of heaven. The veiled nuns stood
around—their loud sobs were heard, even the officiating
priests and brothers wept bitterly; and the "dies iræ"
died away on their quivering lips as the warrior entered.
He flung himself upon the bier, and uttered, in the wild-
ness of his anguish, a thousand maledictions on his
wretched head. It was long before he could be removed,
and then he returned neither to the camp nor court. He
relinquished his mail and helmet for the cowl and gown, and
became a faithful brother of the order of St. Augustine.

Peace be with thee, noble lady; a quiet waiting in the
place of rest, whither thy spirit is departed, for the
summons of thy Lord. This earth has changed greatly
since thy young feet trod the precincts of Sherwood
Forest; the contiguous priory has fallen down, thy
father's castle is still in ruins; all thy companions in the
hall and cloister have passed from the earth; and here,
within this venerable relic of the olden time, in the
midst of a field of corn, reposes thy mortal frame.
Lady Marian—Peace be with thee. Rest in hope, till

the hour of His coming, who shall awake all those who sleep in him, and when, to borrow the beautiful language of inspiration, the groaning creation "shall be delivered from the bondage of corruption into the glorious liberty of the children of God." *

When the Holy One, the Glorious One, returns in might and power,
And the long-oppressed world emerges, from out her darksome hour ;
Her darksome hour of grief, and death, and bitter pain,
When the Holy One, the Blessed One, returns to earth again.

Where the hosts of Satan trod, bright angels shall descend,
And loved ones, and vanished ones, their steps shall hither wend.
They come from the silent land, where they have waited long,
And sweet as mortals never heard shall be their choral song.

We too shall sing with them, for the curse shall pass away,
And earth look brighter far than on her natal day,
When the Lord for whom we waited in glory comes to reign,
And many whom we dearly loved do follow in his train.—M. R.

* Rom. viii. 21.

The Gospel-Tree.

Lone, beside the forest rill,
  Stands an old tree reft and broken;
'Neath its scant boughs waving still,
  Words of faith and hope were spoken,
In time of dearth and bitter woe,
At least six hundred years ago.—M. R.

BRITAIN was anciently divided into a variety of states, which bore the names of those who dwelt in them, or else had reference to some peculiarity of situation or of climate. When the Romans gained the ascendancy, they put aside the way-marks of the olden times, and divided their new territories into Britannia Barbara, Prima, and Secunda, with such lesser partitions as pleased them best. Then came the Saxons.. They, too, made changes, and he who returned after some years' absence to the shores of Britain, sought in vain for the places which he remembered in early life, and with which the dearest associations were connected. The plains and rivers, the hills and valleys, still remained, and above them extended the blue heavens, for men could not dry up the fountain of the one, nor vary the aspect of the other, nor cause the glorious moon and planets to forsake their prescribed bounds. All else was changed. Most of the towns and villages had new names given them, and from out the chaos of war and time arose the seven kingdoms of the Saxon Heptarchy. Minor changes followed, and when Alfred united the whole country under his paternal sway, he projected a final division of the kingdom into counties, with well-defined boundaries and names.

The counties were again divided into parishes, and then commenced the annual festival of marking the respective boundaries. This was done by the inhabitants, who went round them every year, and stopped at certain spots, where different ceremonies were performed, in order that the localities might be impressed on the memory of the young, as they were attested by the recollections of the old. Rogation week, or one of the three days before Holy Thursday, the feast of our Lord's ascension, was selected for the purpose, at which time the minister of the parish, accompanied by his churchwardens and chief parishioners, went round the boundaries, and stopped at remarkable spots and trees, where he recited passages in the gospels, and implored the blessing of the Most High on the fruits of the earth, beseeching Him to preserve the rights and properties of the inhabitants, and to keep them in safety. Many a memorial-tree, thus honoured, carried down the recollec-

tion of bygone days to the men of other generations;
and among these the gospel-beech, which stood at a
short distance from an ancient Saxon town, among the
beautiful beech woods of Gloucestershire, recalled to
mind that ages must have passed since that failing tree,
shadowed with its ample foliage the earth beneath.
Now time-worn and riven, hollow, too, yet throwing out
green leaves in the spring, it marked one of the ex-
tremities of the parish, in its retired coppice on the
rugged side of a wild common, while beside it a stream
gushed forth, and went leaping and sparkling into the
vale below. A variety of flowers grew round the well-
head of the stream, the primrose and the snowdrop, the
yellow daffodil and violet, all young, and fresh, and
lovely, as if in mockery of the time-worn tree. There
stood the parishioners, in their doublets, with heads
uncovered, while the priest recited a few appropriate
sentences from that holy book in which he loved to
instruct them. Playful children, too, were there, young
men and maidens, for on such occasions most of the
parishioners trooped forth, some because they loved
their pastor, and were glad to hear the sacred words that
proceeded from his lips; others because the walk was
pleasant, and to gather the early flowers of the year.
This custom, itself of great antiquity, was conjectured to
be derived from the Pagan feast of Terminalia, the
fabled guardian of fields and landmarks, and the pro-
moter of good fellowship among men. It was adopted

by the Christians during a period of calamity and death, and now a gospel-tree or stone, stands as a memorial in almost every parish. The site was duly visited from year to year, and the doing so was attended with circumstances of peculiar interest. He who had traced the boundaries of his parish with manly step, and who with unwrinkled brow, erect and firm, read the sentences that breathed of confidence and truth, changed with the changing years. When a few years had passed by, it became toil and weariness to him to trace the same rounds. Those who as playful boys, intent on sport, had been thrust into the stream that marked in one place the boundary of the parish, or dragged in another through a coppice, or driven up a tree as if in anger, to make them remember the boundaries, were now grave and thoughtful men, with young striplings beside them. A few years more, and not one of the grown-up people are left. The gospel-tree may remain, but of those who stood as boys or aged men, as young maidens or grave matrons, beneath its shade, some will be laid down in the narrow house, and others will not even present a trace of what they were. Another minister will fill the office of his predecessor, and even the younger children will be grown up to manhood. He who then passes through the village may see old and wrinkled persons looking from their cottage windows, or seated on the green to bless the procession. Those aged persons are strangely altered from what they were. Who may recognise in them, the young men and maidens, who now with joyous hearts and unwearied steps, are pressing round the boundaries!

Thus might have thought and felt the men and women who first stood beside the gospel-tree when the experience of a few short years gave them some little insight into the changes of human life. When not a trace of that company remained, others stood in the same place, and many thought the same among succeeding generations; content to suffer, and to see the breaking asunder of every earthly tie, of all that renders life desirable, while yet the sacred volume declares to those who read and understand, that the present state of human wretchedness is not designed to last for ever.

Ruins of Clipstone Palace.

Where have ye gone, ye statesmen great,
That have left your home so desolate?
Where have ye vanished, king and peer,
And left what ye liv'd for, lying here?
Sin can follow where gold may not,
Pictures and books the damp may rot;
And creepers may hang frail lines of flowers
Down the crevices of ancient towers:
But what hath passed from the soul of mortal,
  Be it thought or word of pride,
Hath gone with him through the dim, low portal,
  And waiteth by his side.—F. W. FABER.

LITTLE now remains of the old palace where King John and Edward I. resided. Creeping ivy covers the once strong walls, and large elder bushes springing from out the rents which time has made, afford a shelter to such birds as like to build their nests in solitary places. The goatsucker is one of these; you may hear her mournful voice at night, as if she bewailed and lamented the downfall of the once stately building; the gray owl is also there; the jackdaw and carrion-crow; they are never seen beside the cottage door, or in cheerful apple-or-

chards, covered with blossoms, where the goldfinch and
linnet, the joyous throstle and the bullfinch, love to
nestle. All is lonely here, the long grass which grows
wild and high, around and within the ruin, is rarely
trodden on, and so damp and chill is the feeling of the
place, that the sheep and cattle that graze upon the
common rarely seek it, unless in the hottest summer-
day, when they cannot find shelter elsewhere. Yet this
lone and melancholy spot was not always thus deserted :
the broken-down walls encircled a spacious area, within
which was all the life and business, the gladness and
festivity of a palace; there was the great hall and the
refectory, the chapel, where prayer was duly offered,
the rooms of state, and apartments of various descrip-
tions. Men-at-arms guarded the strong gate by night
and by day, and when its ample doors were opened by
the king's command, a troop of horse might freely pass,
and large companies did come and go, for great hos-
pitality was occasionally exercised in Clipstone palace.

Fancy, that nimble fairy, who calls up the images of
bygone days, who causes men to live again, and re-
people the fair scenes in which they once rejoiced or
suffered ; who builds up the ruined wall, and removes
the unsightly branches which keep off the pleasant sun-
beams, bids the stately palace of Clipstone to stand
forth in all its majesty. Touched by her wand, the
mists of ages have rolled away, and surely a more
goodly building rarely meets the eye.

The walls are thick, and the embattled parapets present a range of towers, each of which are firmly guarded. The knight or palmer, he who comes in peace or war, has to pass over a strong drawbridge, and through the barbican or watch-tower by which the castle is further strengthened. He sees over his head a portcullis armed with iron spikes like a harrow, and as he passes through the long stone passage, he hears the heavy tread of the guard going their rounds along the high wall, by which the entrance is flanked on either side. The deep moat with its heavy and sluggish waters, the inner and outer ballia, the guard and the portcullis, all and each betoken that the country is in an unsettled state; but within the area on which the castle stands all is bustle and animation, its ample space contains barracks and residences for the workmen attached to the palace, together with a well and chapel, and in the centre stands the keep, where the king presides, and where his great officers have their abode. A terrace walk extends around the keep, and appended to it is a straight bowling-green, where amusements of various kinds are going on. The old castle looks gloomy to him who passes by; it stands an isolated object, stern and lonely, as if nothing within or around it, held communion with any living thing. But such is not the case, for the monarch holds his court here; King John, who has lately come to the throne, and with him is that kind and gentle lady, his fair queen, who tries to soften the rugged temper of her

husband.   Lords of high degree are invited guests;
with them are a large company of knights and squires,
and while tilts and tournaments are going on within the
walls, the retainers of the castle are seen coming with
provisions, or else driving both sheep and cattle, for the
demand for them is great.   Alms are duly given by the
express desire of the queen, and those who seek for shelter
are hospitably entertained.

In winter, the banquet room is lighted up with
large torches, and a band of minstrels make the castle
resound with their songs and roundelays.   You may
hear occasionally the trampling of horses, even when the
company are set at table, and see a number of young
gallants, of knights, too, and minstrels, coming through
the great stone entrance, mounted on steeds richly ca-
parisoned, and clad in fantastic vestments of green and
gold, with high caps and ribands.   Thus accoutred, they
ride round the hall, and pay their respects to the assem-
bled guests with such speeches as best please them.
But torches are not needed now, for summer is at its
height.   Some converse in the great halls, others mount
to the top of the high keep, where they amuse them-
selves with observing the comers and goers from the
castle, and in watching whether any knights or ladies,
mounted on their palfreys, are coming from afar ;
others go forth to hunt over the wild moor, or to chase
the deer in his forest haunts.   Others, again, amuse
themselves with tennis, or foot-ball, or in feats of arms.

Knights and squires are seen going to and fro, conversing on foreign news, or on the valorous achievements of those with whom they are acquainted.

The queen thinks well of such proceedings, and she endeavours to promote the kindly intercourse that subsists within the walls. But now they are put aside. The king is weary of them. The jest and laugh, the discoursing of the old, and the amusements of the young, suit not with his turn of mind or the sad condition of the country. He has other thoughts than those of gladness and festivity, and growing weary of the hospitable life which he is constrained to lead at Clipstone palace, he has suddenly withdrawn from thence and gone to London.

Clipstone looks lonely now. The minstrel's harp is silent, neither knights nor ladies ride forth over the wild moor, and rarely does any one seek for hospitality within the walls. A few men-at-arms guard the place, and you may hear the baying of the watch-dogs at eveningtide; but this is rather from impatience than necessity, for they miss the riders who used to pat their shaggy heads, and speak to them as they passed.

Sad rumours are afloat, but the place is so remote that no one knows what to believe. Some say that a civil war has broken out; others that the country is laid under an interdict, that the church doors are to be closed, and that no one is to be interred in consecrated ground.

A church may be seen among the trees, beside the stream where it forms a small cascade that falls with a pleasant murmur into the vale below. It is a church of the olden time, with its primitive-looking porch, and creeping vine. Prayers have been offered there ever since the days of Alfred, and beside it the villagers have been laid to rest for successive generations : a few bells call the people to their matins and vespers, and some images stand within the walls of the edifice.

Prayers may not be offered now, for the good old priest has received orders to close the doors, and to take down the bells. It is sad to see the few images that have long recalled to recollection the holy lives of those whose memory they are designed to perpetuate, lying with the ancient cross upon the ground, and, as if the air itself is polluted, and may pollute them by its contact, the priest and his attendants carefully cover them, even from their own approach and veneration. The bells, too, which used to ring out, that all might hear and make ready for the house of prayer, are taken down and placed beside the grey tower from whence they had long sounded in seasons of gladness or sorrow. No one hears the passing bell that was wont to call the neighbours to intercede for him who lay weak and sinking upon his bed.

The living partake of no religious rite, except baptism to new-born infants and the communion to the dying ; the dead may not lay in consecrated ground, neither are words of peace, nor any hallowed ceremony spoken or

performed at their obsequies.   Graves are opened beside
the public road, on some wild common, or lone forest ;
those who dig them seem filled with more than usual sad-
ness, for they have not yet learned to think that it is a
matter of indifference where their friends are buried.
Strange it is, that in these fearful times any should
think of marrying.   Yet such there are, and now a bridal
company is seen passing up the narrow pathway that leads
to the small church.   The sun shines as brightly as if all
on earth were happy ; the trees wave in the soft summer
wind, and the butterflies and bees flit from one flower to
another, or rest on the tufts of wild thyme that skirt the
path.   But the old people look exceeding sorrowful,
and there are no smiles on the faces of the young.   They
stop at the entrance of the churchyard, at the old stile
with its thatched roof, where part of the ceremony is wont
to be performed, and the bride and bridegroom stand
there, as if they almost feared to go on.   The sod which
used to be kept so nicely that a weed might not lift up its
head unbidden, has grown long and rank.   It overtops
the graves; and the thistle, and that unsightly weed the
great cow-parsnip, with its sickly-looking flower, has sprung
up in rank luxuriance.   The bells are placed beside the
church, and near them the images, and the one old cross
are lying on the ground, covered up in a manner which
cause them to look like corpses waiting for interment.

In a moment the old church and its venerable yew—
the sad bridal company—the bells and images are gone.

A new scene presents itself, for more than eighty years
have passed since these things were done, and the aspect
of everything is changed.

Clipstone Palace does not look gloomy now.   Altera-
tions have been made, though it is difficult to say how or
where.   There is the keep and the bastion, the wall and
moat, but the place looks lighter, the men-at-arms are
not so heavily loaded with armour, and the knights and
ladies wear a lighter and a gayer dress.   Their palfreys
are elegantly caparisoned, and they go forth with hawks
upon their wrists, and hounds running by their sides, with
only a few attendants.   The dwellings of the poorer classes
are more comfortable than in the days of John, and they
have around them small enclosures, in which grow pot-
herbs, and fragrant flowers.   The country, too, is culti-
vated in many parts, and all look peaceful and contented.

He who surveys the landscape from an eminence,
will observe that houses have been built, which, although
not rising to the dignity of castles, have much of the
ancient baronial style, being strongly moated, and having
the entrance guarded with a portcullis.   They consist of a
quadrangle, with a large area in the centre, into which
both sheep and oxen are often driven for greater security
by night.   The fields around are in general well attended
to, and large gardens, stocked with fruit and vegetables,
supply not only the wants of the respective families, but
also provides abundance of such medicinal herbs, as is
convenient to have within reach.   This style of building

evinces a considerable improvement in society, for during
the insecure condition of the country, when Clipstone
Palace was last brought into view, every baronial residence
was strongly fortified, and scarcely any intermediate
gradations existed between the vassal and his lord, except
in commercial cities.   Men had consequently little
inclination to cultivate the arts of peace.   The knight or
squire who rode forth fully caparisoned, and armed cap-à-
pie, turned not aside his charger into the recesses of the
forest to gather such beautiful flowers as might grow
therein, when there was danger in his path ; the serf, who
toiled hard to sustain his wife and children, had neither
time nor inclination to seek out, or to plant around his
cabin either the wild rose or the honeysuckle.   The
wild rose grew, as now it grows, fragrant and beautiful ;
the honeysuckle, too, and wild flowers of all scents and
hues sprung beside the common, or skirted the thorny
brake ; but the outlaw often lurked among them, and it
was death to him who sought, unarmed or alone, the
beautiful solitude of nature.   But now that the country
is at peace, and the towns and cities contain a class of
persons who grow rich by commerce, and who frequently
obtain in their intercourse with foreign nations, curious
specimens both of art and nature, men begin to lay aside
that dread of their fellow-men which has hitherto caused
them to think most of their personal safety, and to direct
their attention towards improving their own condition.

The dwellings which arose in consequence throughout

the country, and give the traveller a feeling of security
as he passes beside their gardens, or through the path-
ways which lead across the fields, are inhabited by a class
of men who had no political existence in the days of
John. These are the lesser barons. They originated
with the partition of the great estates which had been
given by the Norman conqueror to his immediate fol-
lowers, and which anciently conferred power on indivi-
dual families. Many of these had escheated to the crown
when the heads of them, having taken part in civil broils,
either fell in battle or fled into foreign lands. The king
then generally parcelled such estates among his courtiers
according to their merits; others were divided, either to
make provisions for younger children, or partitioned
among coheirs, and hence originated a number of small
estates, which required economy in the management, and
caused the proprietor to remain much at home, where he
occupied himself in cultivating his paternal or appro-
priated acres, and in attending to his cattle.

It is the wise policy of Edward, who resides much at
Clipstone Palace during the pleasant months of summer,
to encourage and protect the lower orders of society. He
is not ignorant concerning the transactions of other days;
though a long interval has elapsed since the crown was
overawed by the turbulent barons in the days of John;
since that stern and vindictive monarch sat sullenly
brooding over his sad condition, and devising schemes for
aggrandisement or revenge in the same apartment which

King Edward enlivens with his presence; from the embattled parapets of which he can survey the smiling and well-peopled landscape.

A fine young oak grew on the west side of Clipstone Palace in the days of John; it was noticed at that time for its girth and height, and was much admired by many who resided within the park. Parties were assembled occasionally beneath its shade, and the minstrel would wake up his harp in a fine summer evening. Those who loved his lays gathered around him, and while they listened to the deep music that he poured forth, and to the thrilling strains by which it was accompanied, the sun often set below the horizon, and his beams shed a purple light on the rising ground, while the plain country and the woods were covered with the mists of evening. Had the tree a voice, or could its leaves form words when shaken by the wind, how much of ancient history—how many tales of loves and woes—of human suffering and human joys, would be unfolded! The tree looks not now as it did then; somewhat of its grace has passed away, but there is more of majesty; the branches are exceeding ample, and the stem is beginning to be slightly furrowed. Knights and ladies still sit beneath its shade, as in the days of John, and the minstrel's harp is awakened at their bidding, while the same bright sun is setting in his glory behind the hills, on which the inmates of the palace looked in bygone days. The same hopes and joys—the same ties of family and of kindred, were among them as among those of the present day. Modi-

H

fied, indeed, by the times in which they lived—by the hopes or the misgivings of that eventful period, but still the same in all their bearings, on the weal or woe of knight or lady, sire or son.

Now there is another company sitting there; men of grave countenances and full age. Their plaited ruffs and satin doublets, their high-crowned hats and plumes, though reverently laid aside, the richness of their vestments and, above all, their dignified demeanour, show that they are of high degree. Some have broad and ample foreheads, furrowed with deep thought; others seem worn with care; some again appear to have sustained the shock of many battles, and among them are a few with staffs and crosiers, whose countenances denote a life of prayer and abstraction. This goodly company are the counsellors of the king, together with the greater and lesser barons and knights, assembled at his bidding : they hold a parliament beneath the noble tree, for such is the royal pleasure. The king presides in state among them, and right and left, and immediately before him, seats are placed for those whose rank entitles them to the pre-eminence, while the burgesses sit apart. They are deliberating on matters of great importance; on the affairs, perhaps, of Scotland ; for the young Queen Margaret is dead, and the king is devising schemes for obtaining possession of the country. It is a solemn sight to see men thus deliberating, as if eternity depended on their decision, while the very tree beneath which they meet, and the adjacent palace, might teach that human life is even as a vapour.

Gradually as the mist of ages were dispersed, so gradually do they return. They gather over the assembly, and cover, as with a light transparent mantle, the palace with its embattled parapets, and men-at-arms, the moat, and drawbridge. Fainter and fainter grows the scene; the king may yet dimly be discerned, and one among the rest seems speaking with great earnestness; now the strained eye discerns them no longer. All and each are concealed from the view. Where stood the noble oak, and those who were assembled beneath its branches, a solitary spot of ground, with an aged, riven, and time-worn tree, alone appears: in the place of a stately palace, broken ruins meet the eye, and a few straggling sheep graze beside them.

H 2

William Rufus and the Monk of Gloucester.

Ruined Villages in the New Forest.

"The fire from off the hearth hath fled,
    The smoke in air has vanished.
    The last, long, lingering look is given;
    The stifled sigh, and the parting groan,
    And the sufferers on their way are gone."

THE memorial-tree, from which the arrow of Sir Walter
Tyrrel glanced, and beside which the king lay extended
on the ground, is now exceeding old, and scarcely a trace
remains of its former greatness. It stood in this wild
spot, when the stern decree went forth, which enjoined that
throughout the whole extent of the south-western part of
Hampshire, measuring thirty miles from Salisbury to the
sea, and in circumference at least ninety miles, all trace
of human habitation should be swept away. William
might have indulged his passion for the chase in the
many parks and forests which Anglo-Saxon monarchs
had reserved for the purpose, but he preferred rather to
have a vast hunting-ground for his " superfluous and
insatiate pleasure" in the immediate neighbourhood
of Winchester, his favourite place of residence. The
wide expanse that was thus doomed to inevitable desola-
tion was called Ytene or Ytchtene; it comprised nume-
rous villages and homesteads, churches, and ancestral

halls, where Saxon families of rank resided, and where an
industrious population followed the daily routine of pas-
turage and husbandry.*   A large proportion had been
consequently brought into cultivation ; yet sufficient
still remained to afford a harbour for numerous wild
animals.   This part comprised many sylvan spots of
great beauty, with tracts of common land, covered with
the golden blossomed gorse, and tufts of ferns, or else
with short herbage, intermingled with wild thyme.
Noble groups of forest-trees were seen at intervals, with
clear running streams, and masses of huge stones which
projected from among the grass.   The sun rose on the
morning of the fatal day in cloudless beauty, and fresh
breezes tempered the heat, which, at harvest-time
is often great ; the people were already in the fields,
and the creaking of heavy-laden waggons was heard at
intervals, with the sweeping sound of the rapid sickle.
In a moment the scene was changed.   Bands of Norman
soldiers rushed in and drove all before them.   They trod
down the standing corn, and commanded the terrified
inhabitants of hall and hut, to depart in haste.   More
than one hundred manors, villages, and hamlets were
depopulated, even the churches were thrown down—those
venerated places, where the voice of prayer and thanks-
giving had been heard for generations ; where the young
bride pledged her vows, and where words of peace were
spoken to cheer the hearts of those who laid their friends

* Rapin.

to rest beside the walls. He who passed the next day
over the wide waste, saw only ruins black with smoke,
trampled fields, and dismantled churches.   Here and
there broken implements of husbandry met the view,
and beside them, not unfrequently, the corpse of him
who had dared to resist the harsh mandate of the Con-
queror.   Females, too, had fallen to the earth in their
terror and distress, and young children were in their
death-sleep, among the tufts of flowers where they had
sported the day before.   Many stately buildings were
pulled down at once; others, having their roofs thrown
open, were left to be destroyed by the weather, and
hence it not seldom happened that a stranger, in passing
through a meadow into one of those shady coverts, which
still varied the aspect of the country, forgetting, in the
freshness and the loveliness of all around him, the
terrible undoings of previous days, might see through the
undulating branches of the trees, the walls or roofs of
houses, which looked as if they had escaped the general
ruin.   They stood, apparently, in the midst of cultivated
fields, occasionally by the road side, and their pointed
roofs were covered with the vine or honeysuckle.   On a
nearer approach the illusion vanished, not a sound dis-
turbed the silence of the place; the houses which looked
so inviting when seen at a short distance, showed that the
hand of ruin had done its work.   The doors were broken
open, the windows dashed in, the roofs were open to the
winds of heaven, and the little gardens overrun with

weeds.   Large rents appeared in the walls, which were generally made of wood, neatly plastered, and he who looked through the breaches saw that tufts of rank grass, had grown up in the spaces between the stones, with which the floors were occasionally paved.   The ruins of an antique abbey were often close at hand, with its richly painted windows, broken through and through; or, perhaps, the shattered walls of some hospitable dwelling, in which a Saxon thane had resided.   The open space before the house, where, in summer weather, the family used to assemble, where the harp was heard, and the young people amused themselves with sports of various kinds, was overrun with weeds.   There was no print of footsteps on the grass, no trace that the place had recently been inhabited; those who once lived there had found another home; perhaps the low and silent one which alone remains for the houseless and the miserable.

It was said of the proud Norman, that he loved wild beasts as if he had been their father.   He enacted laws for their preservation, which tended to render him extremely unpopular, and while the slaying of a man might be atoned for by a moderate compensation, it was decreed, that whoever should kill a stag or deer, a wild boar, or even a hare, should be punished with total blindness.*   Even the Norman chiefs, who were in general great lovers of the chase, were prohibited from keeping sporting dogs on their own estates unless they subjected

* M. Paris.

the poor animals to such a mutilation of their fore-paws as rendered them unfit for hunting. This enactment pressed hard upon the Norman and English barons, for many of them depended chiefly for subsistence on their bows and nets.

Where the labour of man has ceased, vegetation soon asserts her empire, and fields, when left to themselves, become, according to their soil, either wild or stony, or else covered with a dense growth of underwood, and tall trees. Such was the case over the wide expanse which had been rendered desolate ; the spaces of common ground, with golden blossomed gorse and wild thyme, continued such as they had been, but trees grew thick and fast, the beautiful groves became woods in the course of a short time, and the once cultivated country was rapidly absorbed in the wilderness portions of Ytchtene. A vast forest darkened the land, and all trace of ruined homes and dismantled churches disappeared in many parts, while in others, either the line of erections might be traced by the elevation of the soil, or else large blocks of stone, and here and there a broken arch, or doorway, long pointed out the site of a church or castle. Names, too, are even now retained, with the recollection of their own sad histories. Church-place and Church-moore seems to mark the solitary spots as the sites of ancient buildings, where the Anglo-Saxons worshipped and dwelt in peace, before the stern decree of the unrelenting conqueror razed the sacred edifices. Thompson's

Castle recalls to mind, the cheerfulness and hospitality that presided in an ancestral hall, while the termination of *ham* and *ton*, annexed to many of the woodlands, may be taken as an evidence that where innumerable boughs are waving, a thronging population once inhabited.

The memorial-tree, which now stands lone and seamed, was then a sapling, for such we may conjecture to have been the case, according to the well-known longevity of forest-trees.   Three events of great interest are associated with it—the making desolate a wide extent of country; the death of the proud Norman, by whose command the work of ruin was achieved; and the untimely end of his successor.

Had the history of William I. been written with reference to his private actions, it might be noticed that a tissue of domestic sorrows succeeded to the laying desolate of Ytchtene.   His wife Matilda died a few years after, and his fair daughter Gundreda, the cherished one in her father's house, was cut off in the flower of her youth.   He saw with grief the jealousy that subsisted between his sons William and Henry, and during the time that Duke Robert, his first-born, continued an exile and a fugitive, Richard, his second son, was gored to death by a stag, as he was hunting over the wide expanse which his father had depopulated.   Men spoke of the sad event as a just punishment on him who had respected neither the lives nor feelings of those who once had dwelt there.   Some said, this is but one;

we shall see others of his family to whom the forest will
prove fatal, and they spoke true.

War was declared with France, and a gathering of the
bandit chiefs who had accompanied the king from
Normandy, with their sons, and all who held of him a
fief, was convened at Sarum.   Thither, accordingly,
they came, barons and men-at-arms, abbots and their
vassals, to the number of six thousand, all bound to do
service to the king, and having oaths of homage and
allegiance tended to them in the place of their assem-
bling, that both those who went, and such as remained
behind, might afresh remember to do his bidding.
Sarum was well suited for the purpose, both on account
of its accommodations, and the fine downs by which it
was surrounded.   It was anciently a place of considerable
note, at first a Roman station, afterwards the residence
of the Emperor Severus.

When the assembly which had met at Sarum was
dissolved, the king returned to London, whence he
shortly afterwards departed for the continent, taking
with him his two sons, and a " mighty mass of money,"
as wrote one who lived at the time, " piled together for
some great attempt," and followed by the execrations of
his Saxon subjects.   The object of the expedition was
expressly to take possession of the city of Mantes, with
a rich territory situated between the Epte and the Oise.
It is needless to speak of the negociations with which
the French king endeavoured to amuse his rival, while

he secretly authorized his barons to make excursions on the frontiers of Normandy; or of the deadly hatred which induced William to delay his attack on Maine till the approach of autumn made his vengeance more dreadful to the country. The corn was nearly ready for the sickle, and the grapes hung in ripening clusters on the vines, when the fierce king ordered his men to advance on the devoted territory; when in the bitterness of his spirit he marched his cavalry through the corn-fields, and caused his soldiers to tear up the vines, and cut down the pleasant trees. Mantes could offer but a weak resistance, and the town was set on fire. This was the last scene of the tragedy in which the Norman conqueror had acted a conspicuous part; which commenced on the battle-field of Hastings, and ended in the monastery of St. Gervas. Riding beside the ruined town, to view the misery which he had wrought, his horse trod on some hot cinders; the frightened creature plunged violently, and the king being unable to retain his seat, fell to the ground. The injury which he sustained caused him to be carried in a litter to a religious house, in the neighbourhood of Rouen, where his army was encamped, for he could not bear, he said, the noise of the great city. It was told by those who were present at the time, that although he at first preserved much apparent dignity, and conversed calmly on the events of his past life, and concerning the vanity of human greatness; when death drew near,

the case was otherwise. He then spoke and felt as a
dying man, who was shortly to appear before the
tribunal of his Maker, there to render an account of all
the deeds which he had done, of all the gifts committed
to his care, of his riches and his power. His hard
heart softened then, and he bitterly bewailed the
cruelties which he had committed. He thought of the
fair city which he had ordered to be set in flames, and
though he could not bring to life the many who
had fallen in the dreadful day of its undoing, nor soothe
the mental anguish which that day had caused, he sent
a messenger in haste with a large sum for the rebuilding
of the monasteries and churches. The noble patrimony
which he had wrested from ill-fated Harold, was con-
sidered with other thoughts than those with which he left
the shores of England. A large sum was also remitted to
the religious houses, that he might obtain remission for the
robberies which he had committed there. Some who
waited beside his couch suggested that whoever sought
for mercy at the hand of the Most High, must show
mercy to his fellow-men, and they entreated him to
remember the unhappy persons who had pined for
many years in their lone prison-houses, shut out from all
the privileges of social life. The fierce king felt that it
was easier to give money for rebuilding churches
than pardon to an enemy; and it was not till he appre-
handed his last hour to be close at hand, that he gave
orders for releasing the state-prisoners. The Earls of

Moriar, of Beron, and Ulnot, the brother of Harold, were accordingly set at liberty ; and the Norman, Roger Fitz Osborn, formerly Earl of Hereford, with Odo, the turbulent Bishop of Bayeux, also received permission to leave their respective prisons, although the king remarked with reference to the latter, that by so doing he was letting loose a firebrand, that might desolate both England and Normandy.

One morning early, the chief prelates and barons received a summons to assemble with all haste in the chamber of the king, who finding his end approach, desired to finish the settlement of his affairs. They came accordingly, though the day had not yet dawned, and found with him his two sons, Henry and William, who waited impatiently for the declaration of his will. " I bequeath the duchy of Normandy," said he, " to my eldest son Robert. As to the crown of England, I bequeath it to no one, for I did not receive it, like the duchy of Normandy, from my father, but acquired it by conquest, and the shedding of blood, with mine own sword. The succession of that kingdom, I therefore, leave to the decision of the Almighty. My own most fervent wish is, that my son William, who has ever been dutiful to me in all things, may obtain and prosper in it." " And what do you give me, O my father ?" impatiently cried Prince Henry, who had not been mentioned. " Five thousand pounds weight of silver out of my treasury," was his answer.

" But what can I do with five thousand pounds of silver, if I have neither lands nor a home ? " " Be patient," rejoined the king, " and have trust in the Lord; suffer thy elder brothers to precede thee—thy time will come after theirs." On hearing this, Prince Henry hurried off to secure the silver, which he weighed with great care, and then provided himself with a strong coffer, having locks and iron bindings to keep his treasure safe. William, also, staid no longer by the bed-side of his dying parent; he called for his attendants, and hastened to the coast, that he might pass over without delay to take possession of his crown. He, whose sword had made many childless, was thus deserted in his hour of greatest need by his unnatural sons.

The sun had scarcely risen over the plains of Rouen, and scarcely had his beams lighted the lofty pinnacles of the church and abbey, when the conqueror was roused from his stupor by the sound of the church bell. Eagerly inquiring what the sound meant, he was answered that they were tolling the hour of prime, in the church of St. Mary. On hearing this, he seemed to revive for a few moments, and then suddenly lifting up his hands, he cried aloud, " I recommend my soul to my Lady Mary, the holy mother of our Lord !" having thus said, he sunk back and expired.

> What busy meddling thoughts had power
> To haunt him e'er that solemn hour,

What broken thoughts of by-gone days,
Visions of youth, and welcome lays,
Lays, that the harp could soothly sound,
When merry steps went pranking round.
And then his father's castle hall,
And sooth and bland the cheerful call,
Of voices lov'd in distant clime,
Were seen and heard at that sad time;
Lov'd forms did round his pillow bend,
And gentle hands his bidding tend,
The wife and mother by his side,
In bloom of youth and beauty's pride,
His own dear child, Gundreda fair,
With gentle step and smile was there;
But soon the fitful dream was gone,
The dying man was all alone,
Save that stern men were waiting round,
With cowl and casque, and helm unbound.—M. R.

His last sigh was a signal for a general flight and
scramble. The knights buckled on their spurs, the
priests and doctors, who had passed the night by his
bed-side, made no delay in leaving their wearisome
occupation. " To horse ! to horse !" resounded through
the monastery, and each one galloped off to his own
home, in order to secure his interests or his property.
A few of the king's servants, and some vassals of minor
rank staid behind, but not to do honour to the poor
remains of him who had been their king. They spoke
loudly and trod heavily, where but a short time before
men would scarcely have dared to whisper; where the
noiseless step and hushed sound, told the rank and
sufferings of him, whom now the voice of seven thunders

would not wake. They proceeded without remorse to rifle the apartment both of arms and silver vessels; they even took away the linen and royal vestments, and having hastily packed them in bundles, each man threw the one, which he secured, upon his steed, and galloped away like the rest. From six till nine the corpse of the mighty conqueror lay on the bare boards, with scarcely a sheet to cover him. One son was gone, the other was looking to his pelf, his officers and men-at-arms, priests and doctors had deserted him; the queen, who would have watched beside his dying couch, and soothed his restless pillow, who dearly loved him whilst living, and would not have forsaken him when dead, was herself in the still grave. His favourite and youngest daughter, had likewise been laid to rest, and Eleanor, Margaret, Alela, Constance, and Cecilia were far distant. Here, then, lay the corpse of William in the dismantled apartment, while the men of Rouen, who were thrown into the greatest consternation by the event of the king's death, hurried about the streets, asking news of one another, or advice concerning the present emergency, or else busied themselves in hiding such things as were most valuable. At length the monks and clergy recollected the condition of the deceased monarch, and forming a procession, they went with a crucifix and lighted tapers to pray over the dishonoured body. The Archbishop of Rouen wished that the interment should take place at Caen, in preference to his own city, it being thought most proper that the church of St.

Stephen, which the king had built, and royally endowed, should be honoured with his sepulchre. But there was no one to give orders concerning the obsequies of him who had been so great on earth; his sons and brothers, every relation, and all the chiefs who had shared his favours were away. Not one was found even to make inquiry respecting the interment, excepting a poor knight who lived in the neighbourhood, and who charged himself with the trouble and expense of the funeral, " out of his natural good nature, and love of the Most High." Arrangements were made accordingly, and the corpse being carried by water to Caen, was received by the abbots and monks of St. Stephen, while the inhabitants of the city, having formed a procession, headed by the neighbouring ecclesiastics, proceeded towards the abbey. Suddenly a fire broke out, and each one, whether priest or layman, running to his home or monastery to prevent the spreading of the flames, the brothers of St. Stephen alone remained with the bier. Onward, then, they went, and there was somewhat of funereal solemnity in the last sad act, for mitred abbots in their robes, with bishops and ecclesiastics in their gowns and cowls, stood within the abbey walls, in order to receive the corpse. Mass was then performed, the Bishop of Evreux pronounced a panegyric on him who had borne the name of Conqueror while living, and who had done great deeds among his fellow-men, and the bier on which lay the body of the king, attired in royal robes, and being in no respect concealed from the view, was about to be lowered into the grave, when a stern voice forbade the interment. " Bishop," it said, " the man whom you have praised was a robber. The very ground on which we are standing is mine; and this is the site of my father's house. He took it from me by violence to build this church upon its ruins. I reclaim it as my right, and in the name of the Most High I forbid you to bury him there, or to cover him with my glebe." The man who spoke thus boldly, was Asseline Fitz-Arthur. He had vainly sought for justice from the king while living, and he loudly proclaimed the fact of his injustice and oppression, before his face, when dead. It seemed fearful to the bystanders, that the funeral should thus be strangely hindered; that as at first no one had cared to bury him, whose pale, shrunk countenance and lifeless form was still upheld above the grave; when some at length were gathered, who thought to do him honour, the most were hurried off by an alarm of fire, and that at the very moment of his interment, even the solemn act could not proceed in peace. Many who were present well remembered the pulling down of Fitz-Arthur's house, and the distress which it occasioned, and the bishop being assured of the fact, gave his son, sixty shillings for the grave alone, and engaged to procure the full value of his land. One moment more, and the corpse remained among living men; another, and it disappeared in the darkness of the tomb, and the remainder of the ceremony being hurried over, the assembly broke up in haste.

" The red king lies in Malwood Keep.
　To drive the deer o'er lawn and steep,
　　He's bound him with the morn;
　His steeds are swift, his hounds are good,
　　The like in covert or high wood,
　Were never cheered with horn."—W. STEWART ROSE.

Barons and men-at-arms were assembled in Malwood-Keep, at the invitation of William Rufus, who proposed to hold a chase, and to follow the red-deer over the wide hunting-grounds, where once stood the pleasant homes, which his father had rendered desolate.　Prince Henry was there also, and he who passed at nightfall might have heard loud shouts of revelry resounding from the castle, while the bright light which streamed from the windows, gave a strange effect to the giant shadows, which the tall trees of the dark forest cast on the greensward. A loud cry was heard that night which awakened all who slept, and caused them to start in terror from their beds; it came from the king's chamber, whose voice resounding through the castle, loudly invoked the blessed Virgin, and called in great fear for lights to be brought immediately.　He told those who hastened to his assistance that he had seen a hideous vision, and he enjoined them to pass the night at his bed-side, and to divert him with pleasant converse, lest being left alone, the vision should appear again.　At length the morning began to dawn, and the forest which had looked so gloomy at nightfall was gloriously lighted up with the bright beams of an August sun; no strange mysterious-looking shadows caused the passer-by to feel afraid; but instead

of these, waving branches gently rustled in the morning
breeze, and the cheerful songs of early birds resounded
from the thickets. William began to prepare for the
chase, and while he was thus employed, an artizan
brought him six new arrows. He praised their work-
manship, and putting aside four for himself, he gave the
other two to Sir Walter Tyrrel, or, as he was often called,
Sir Walter de Poix, from his estates in France, saying,
as he presented them, " Good weapons are due to him,
who knows how to make a right use of them." The
breakfast-tables were plentifully supplied, and those who
sat around them, talked of the expected pleasures of the
chase, while the red king ate and drank even more than
he was· wont.   Perhaps the fearful vision of the night still
troubled him, and he sought to put aside the recollection ;
for it was observed that his spirits rose at length to the
highest pitch. Malwood-Keep resounded with merriment
as it had done the night before, and the horses were seen
standing ready saddled, with hounds in leashes, and
grooms and huntsmen preparing for the chase.   Many
of the younger barons were already mounted, and their
horses were curvetting on the grass, as though they partook
of the impatience of their riders, while every now and then
the blast of the hunter's horn, in the hand of some young
squire, gave notice to those within, that the sun was
already high.   All was gaiety and animation, and bois-
terous mirth within and around Malwood-Keep, when a
stranger was seen approaching through the forest, grave,

and yet in haste. He spoke as one who had business of moment to communicate, and which admitted of no delay, but his look and voice sufficed to check the eagerness of those who sought to know whence, and why, he came. He told the king, when admitted to his presence, that he had travelled both far and fast; that the Norman abbot of St. Peter's at Gloucester had sent to inform his majesty how greatly he was troubled on his account, for that one of his monks had dreamed a dream which foreboded a sudden and awful death to him.—" To horse !" hastily exclaimed the king, " Walter de Poix, do you think that I am one of those fools who give up their pleasure, or their business, for such matters ? the man is a true monk, he dreameth for the sake of money ; give him an hundred pence, and bid him dream of better fortune to our person."

Forth went the hunting train, and while some rode one way, some another, according to the manner adopted in the chase, Sir Walter de Tyrrel, the king's especial favourite, remained with him, and their dogs hunted together. They had good sport, and none thought of returning, although the sun was sinking in the west and the shadows of the forest-trees began to lengthen on the grass, at which time an hart came bounding by, between the king and his companion, who stood concealed in a thicket. The king drew his bow, but the string broke, and the arrow took no effect; the hart being startled at the sound, paused in his speed, and looked on all sides, as if doubtful which way to turn. The king, meanwhile gazing steadfastly at the creature, raised his bridle-hand above his eyes, that he might shade them from the glare of the sun, which now shone almost horizontally through the forest, and being unprovided with a second bow, he called out "Shoot Walter, shoot away!"* Tyrrel drew his bow, but the arrow went not forth in a straight line, it glanced against a tree, and struck the king in its side-course against his breast, which was left exposed by the raised arm. The fork-head pierced his heart, and in an instant he expired. No words were spoken, no prayer passed his lips; one dismal groan alone was heard, and the red king lay extended on the grass.† Sir Walter flew to his side, but he saw that his master was beyond all human aid, and mounting his horse he hastened to the sea-coast, from whence he embarked for Normandy. He was heard of soon after, as having fled into the dominions of the French king, and the next account of him was, that he had gone to the Holy Land.

Popular superstition had long darkened the New Forest with awful spectres; it was even said that words were heard in its deepest solitudes, of awful import, denouncing vengeance on the Norman and his evil counsellors. This was not strange, for men could still remember the driving out of the unoffending population; the traces of their dwellings might be seen at intervals, and many a broken cross denoted where a church had

* Hen. Knyghton.

† A small silver cross of beautiful workmanship was found buried a few years since, near the fatal tree.

I

stood. The human mind naturally recoils from scenes of horror, and few were bold enough to visit even the outskirts of the forest, at nightfall, and alone. A son of Duke Robert was killed while hunting in the forest by a random arrow, and now again the blood of the Conqueror was poured on the site of an Anglo-Saxon church, which the father of him who lay extended on the earth had pulled down.* Rufus had left the bed-side of his dying parent while life still lingered, intent only on obtaining the English crown; he even left the care of his interment to the hands of strangers, for it does not seem that he at all concerned himself about the matter. Now then was he also left alone, in the depth of the still forest. Walter Tyrrel, intent only on effecting his escape, or else bewildered by the suddenness of the calamity, did not seek for any one to assist in burying him; his companions in the chase were eagerly following their amusement, and chanced not to pass where he was lying. At length the royal corpse was discovered by a poor charcoal-burner, who put it, still bleeding, into his cart, and drove off to Winchester. The intelligence soon spread, and Henry hastened to seize the treasures that belonged to the crown, while the knights, who had reassembled at Malwood-Keep, thought only how the accident might affect themselves; no one caring to show respect to the remains of the unhappy monarch, with whom they had banquetted the evening before. It was afterwards observed

* Mentioned by Walter Hennyngforde, and quoted in Grafton's Chronicle.

by many, that as the corpse of the Conqueror lay extended
on a board, with scarcely a vestment to cover him,
so, by a remarkable coincidence, the body of his
unnatural son, unwashed, without even a mantle, and
hideous to look upon, remained in the cart of the
charcoal-burner till the next day, when it was conveyed
in the same condition to the cathedral church of Win-
chester.   There, however, some faint show of respect
was paid to what had been a king : it was interred in
the centre of the choir, where, as wrote the chronicler of
this sad history, many persons looked on, but few
grieved.   It was even said by some, that the fall of a
high tower which covered his tomb with ruins, showed
the just displeasure of Heaven against one, who having
deserted his dying parent, sought not to repair the evils
which he had done, who neither acting justly, nor living
righteously, was undeserving of Christian burial.

The Old Trees in Hyde Park.

" What are the boasted palaces of man,
   Imperial city or triumphal arch,
   To the strong oak, that gathers strength from time
   To grapple with the storm? Time watch'd
   The blossom on the parent bough. Time saw
   The acorn loosen from the spray. Time pass'd,
   While springing from its swad'ling shell, yon oak,
   The cloud-crowned monarch of the woods, up sprang
   A royal hero from his nurse's arms.
   Time gave it seasons, and time gave it years,
   Ages bestow'd, and centuries grudg'd not;
   Time knew the sapling when gay summer's breath

> Shook to the roots the infant oak, which after
> Tempests moved not.   Time hollow'd in its trunk
> A tomb for centuries ; and buried there
> The epochs of the rise and fall of states,
> The fading generations of the world,
> The memory of man."

HYDE PARK was covered in ancient times with a dense growth of tall trees and underwood, which extending from sea to sea, shaded a large portion of the states of the Iceni and Trinobantes, the Cantii and the Regni. But the aspect of external nature has changed since ; instead of noble trees and all the varied undulations of innumerable boughs, now gently waving in the breeze of summer, and now furiously wrought upon by the northern blast, great London has arisen where all was wood and swamp, and on the space which still retains somewhat of the character that once it bore, are all the accompaniments of a modern park.   Clumps of trees, arranged by the hand of taste, flowering shrubs, and beautifully tufted groves, delight the eye with their beauty or their fragrance ; walks and carriage-drives, lead among them, and through that portion, which bears especially the name of park, winds a gentle river, which reflects on its mirror-like waters, green sloping banks, where cattle graze.

An aged tree grows on the right hand of the road, beside the river, with its trunk devoid of bark, and cracked in all directions, the effect of long exposure to the wea- ther.   Its bare and skeleton-looking branches are also

without bark, and beside it stands another tree, the twin
brother of its desolation.   These trees are very aged, for
the oldest inhabitant in the neighbourhood remembers to
have seen them in the same condition when he climbed
their trunks, a playful boy in search of the owl's nest; but
she was too wary to confide her young to so poor a
shelter.

Those who, in their haste, wish to accomplish the
designs which they have projected with too precipitate haste,
may derive a moral lesson from these once noble trees.
Each was once enfolded within an auburn nut, a cup and
ball that babes might play with, and which the joyous
squirrel, when seeking her food, might have carried off
with ease; and nibbled in a moment all the delicate
ramifications, and the embryo vastness of the future tree.
Autumnal rains mellowed the ground on which the
acorns were deposited, we know not whether by the hand
of man, or whether, dropping from a bough before the
forest had disappeared from the moor, some skipping deer,
dibbling the soft earth with his pointed hoof, prepared a
receptacle in which the acorns might rest secure, till the
return of spring.   Here then lay the auburn nuts.
Leaves reft by the winds of Autumn fell thick and fast
upon the earth, and over them the snow formed a light
covering; and though the wind howled in its fury, and
the heavy storm raged through the forest, the acorns
remained safe till the winds ceased their contention, and
the storm-clouds passed by.   Then did the acorns open

by virtue of that secret and mighty power which re-clothes the forest-boughs with leaves, and causes the herbless soil, to be covered with grass and flowers. Two small lobes first uprose from out the soil, formed with the exactest symmetry, and being in themselves both thick and well furnished with pores, they served not only to shield the small buds that lay between them, but to yield abundant moisture for the support of their nascent life. Presently a young leaf emerged from the bud, then the leaf was pushed upwards by the supporting stem, till at length other small leaves appeared, and the character of a tree was gradually assumed. Meanwhile the tender scions were watered with early dews, and warmed by a bright sun; the rain fell on them, and the internal heat which had preserved life within the acorns, while they lay embedded in the cold earth, did its work, and the trees advanced in their growth.

What people inhabited Britain when these things were being done? Were they the natives of the island, or were they Romans, Danes, or Saxons, Picts or Scots? Did the rude dwellings of our remotest ancestors skirt the margin of the forest on the plain country? did their woad-dyed chieftains walk beneath the parent trees; or the Druid cut with his golden knife, the hallowed misletoe from their branches? Were the gentle undulations of hill and dale varied with palaces and forums? did the Roman dwell among them, or were they trod upon by the ruthless Dane, or the proud Norman, when the trees attained

to their maturity ?   No spirit dwells within their trunks,
as the poets feigned concerning their brethren of Dodona ;
no voice answers to the question.   The sighing of the
wind alone is heard among their sapless branches.

Thus much we know, that in all forest-trees the stages
of vegetation are alike.   But century after century must
have rolled on, till the giant bulk of the noble trees were
fully developed, till their stately columns, upheld an
ample canopy of spreading boughs, beneath which the
flocks that grazed in the open spaces of the forest might
find a shelter from the storm.   Time was, when the settling
of a fly upon the saplings could shake them to the root,
but at this period of their history, a tempest would not disturb
them.   The busiest thoughts might find an ample field to
range in, when comparing the small beginnings, with the
matchless grandeur of these once noble trees.   How, at
their prime age, the smooth bark, by which they were
enveloped, contained within their girth, wood sufficient to
plank the deck and sides of a large vessel; how their
tortuous arms would have yielded many a load of timber,
which, if drawn by oxen, might have wearied the pon-
derous creatures, long before they reached the place of
destination, at even a short distance.   But, in those ages,
oaks were not hewn down as they now are.   Still the
trees grew on, till their moss-cushioned roots upheaved
above the earth, and their smooth trunks, becoming
rugged, were embossed with globose wens.   Then
decay began her noiseless work; one atom, and then

another, were silently disjointed from the rest, till at
length a labour was achieved in the breaking down of
these firm trees, which, had it been done by the hand
of man, would have made the wide forest ring. Nothing
now remains of the once gigantic trees, not even the sem-
blance of their ancient selves—nothing but shapeless trunks,
heavy ponderous masses, with here and there a strip of
rugged bark, in the interstices of which, tufts of moss and
pendent ferns have struck their roots. There is nothing
either in the trunks or branches to tempt the woodman's
hatchet, and therefore, the old trees still remain. Their
roots are firmly interlaced in the earth, they clasp the
blocks of stone that lie buried beneath the soil, with
their stout spurs and knotted fangs, while here and there
a projecting mass rises above the scanty herbage, dotted
over with the yellow lichen and little nailwort which
grows on dry walls and rocks. Crooked into every ima-
ginable shape, they still hold their stems erect, memorials
of past ages, revealers of what time has done;—yea, per-
haps, also what the hand of man has achieved, though the
old trees stand not, as many others, chroniclers connected
with some of those memorable events, which give a date to
history, and are waymarks, which identify the noiseless
steps of time. The winds of many winters have reft off the
giant branches which long since afforded a shelter from the
blast; rovers of the forest—men, perhaps, with bow and
shaft, have burnt them. Some have left, in breaking, a
bleached and splintered stump, but concerning others

there is no trace even of the branch on which they grew;
rough bark has grown most probably over it, and moss
and tufted lichens have taken root in the interstices.
Still, life lingers in the worn-out trees, and proofs are not
wanting, that its secret and mighty power is yet working,
though death preponderates.   The passer-by sees with as-
tonishment, young green leaves in the interstices of the
quarried bark; he sees them, but can hardly believe that
the shapeless thing which stands before him has life hidden
where all seems to denote death; that her sweet force is
equally available in the furrowed oak, as among the young
green trees of the neighbouring coppice, which sprung, it
may be, from out the earth, a thousand years later, in the
lapse of time.

The old trees are well qualified by age, to teach lessons
of wisdom to hoary men.   Had they a voice, they could
discourse much concerning the mutability of things below;
how nations have risen and waned, while they advanced
to maturity, and of the gradual emerging of a mighty
people from the darkness of past ages, to the highest pitch
of intellectual culture.   But this may not be, for the
gifts of speech and reason, of voice and memory, are not
for these ancient tenants of the soil.   Leaning against their
mossy trunks, with no prompter, and no hearer, except
the time-worn trees and the calm still scene around me,
let me be myself the oracle, and discourse to mine own
ear, concerning the mutations of past ages.

Here, then, in bye-gone days, stood one vast forest,

with its dells and dingles, its clear prattling streams, and ceaseless murmur of wind among the branches. We know not that men dwelt within its precincts, or that the natives of the country, our remotest ancestors, built their wattled dwellings, or fed their flocks in the open spaces; most probably not, for the wild animals that ranged here were dangerous to contend with. Years went on, and men clad in skins, and dyed blue with woad, came from the shores of Gaul. They established themselves in the plain country which is bounded by the British Channel, and formed at length a considerable settlement beside the river that waters this part of Britain. They also threw up bulwarks, and added to the natural strength of the place by forming ramparts and sinking fosses. The settlement was called Llyn-din, or the town on the lake, Llyn being the British term for a broad expanse of water or lake. It was appropriately given, for the low grounds on the Surrey side of the river were often overflowed, as also those that extend from Wapping marsh to the Isle of Dogs, and still further, for many miles along the Essex coast. At length, strangers from another country settled there. They saw that the land was good, and that the trees which crowded around the settlement, and shadowed on either side the current of the river, might be cleared away. They were men who soon carried into execution the schemes which they devised, and having enlarged the place, and raised within it noble buildings, for beauty and security, they gave it the name of Londinium.

A fort was built, and ships came from a distance, bring-
ing with them the productions of other climes. Then
began the trees of the great forest to fall beneath the axe
of the woodcutter, and the marshy places were brought
into cultivation. Londinium rapidly advanced to the
dignity of a military station; it even became the capital
of one of the great provinces, into which the Romans
divided Britain.

A spirit of enterprise had ever characterised the polished
people who now gained an ascendency; not only were
the marshy places in the forest drained for the purpose
of feeding cattle, but the low-ground which lay along the
river, and which, in rainy seasons, presented an unsightly
aspect, was recovered from the waters. Embankments
were thrown up on either side to prevent the encroach-
ments of the tide. They commenced in what are now
St. George's Fields, and continued along the adjoining and
equally shallow marshes, till they terminated in the grand
sea-wall of the deep fens of Essex. Thus, in compara-
tively a short period, those vast tracts of land which
presented, during winter, only a dreary expanse of
troubled waters; in the summer, small stagnant pools,
with a dry crust of mud, and here and there tufts of
rushes, or rank grass, were covered with splendid villas,
and a thronging population.

The giant work of embanking the river was succeeded by
making one of those great military roads which opened a
communication from one end of the island to the other.

This was the old Watling or Gathelin Street: it led from London to Dover, and was much travelled on by those who were going to embark for the Imperial city. The making of the road broke up the quiet of the forest, through an extent of which it had to pass; nothing was heard but the crashing of noble trees, and the rattling of cars, heavily laden with stone and lime ; it was carried within sight of the old trees, and, having crossed what is now the Oxford road, at Cumberland-gate, it ran to the west of Westminster, over the river Thames, and onward into Kent. This was its broad outline, and the country through which it lay had been reclaimed either from the forest or the river. It was exceedingly frequented, and carriages of all descriptions continually passed and repassed, either in going to, or else returning from the city.

Londinium was next surrounded with a wall, and a considerable extent of forest-land was cleared for the purpose of being enclosed within its ample range. It was said that the mother of Constantine, who liked much to reside in the rising city, greatly favoured this great work, and that she urged her son to promote the grandeur and security of the place. The wall encompassed the city from right to left. It began at the fort, which occupied a portion of what is now the Tower, and made a circuit of nearly two miles, and one furlong. Another wall, strongly defended with towers and bastions, extended along the banks of the river, to the distance of one mile, and one hundred and twenty yards. The height of the wall was twenty two feet, that of the towers forty feet, and the space of ground enclosed within the circumference of both walls, was computed at three hundred and eighty acres.

Thus stood Londinium. Patricians and military officers, merchants and artificers, resorted thither from all parts, and there Constantine held his court, with the splendour of Imperial Rome. A few more years, and the power of the Romans began to wane, and with it waned also, the prosperity of the sea-girt isle. Stranger barks came from the shores of Saxony, and in them armed men of fierce countenances, who knew little of the arts of civilized life. What they saw, they conquered, and the noble city with its palaces and forums, its schools, of eloquence, and temples for Pagan worship, fell into their hands. Then might be seen from the old trees the red glare of the burning city; but it was again rebuilt, and though, in after years, the Danes sorely oppressed its inhabitants, it resumed its high standing as the metropolis of Britain; the seat of arts and commerce; kings reigned within its walls, and merchants came from all parts of the known world, bringing with them the productions of other countries, and exciting a spirit of enquiry and enterprise, throughout all classes of society.

The old trees remained as they were, and London, for so the city was called at length, increased in might and power; the swarming population could no longer be contained within its walls, and the walls were broken down in consequence. Villages were built in places where, but a few years before, was a dense growth of underwood, with high trees that cast their lengthened shadows on the ground.　Gradually the city enlarged her bounds, and those groups of houses which had been called villages, and which stood in the midst of pleasant fields, well-watered and reclaimed from the forest, were reached by lines of streets, and so encroaching were they, that it was thought advisable to retain some portion of the ancient forest as a royal park, both for exercise and ornament.　If the trees of the forest could have spoken, they would have rejoiced at this, but none more than the old trees, my own memorial trees, these relics of past ages; though now beginning to decay, long tufts of lichens having struck their roots into the rough bark, and many of their noblest branches having been long since broken by fierce winds, or rovers of the forest.　They nearly stood alone, for very few remained of those which had grown here, when all around was one wide forest, one intermingling of shadowing boughs from sea to sea, or spaces of waste land, untilled and tenantless.　The old Roman road, which had been raised with so much cost and care, soon fell to decay; its materials were carried off, and the green sward rapidly extended over that portion of it which passed through Hyde Park and St. James's Park.　Those who like to tread where the Romans trod, may yet walk on a small portion of their ancient route, in the public road leading to Westminster Abbey, on the side nearest the turnpike.

The retaining part of the old forest was a desirable measure, for the advance of London towards this quarter, was alone restrained by the prescribed boundaries; and now the windows of her crowding houses look upon the trees and grass, and the ceaseless hum of human voices, which she sends forth from all her hundred gates, is heard continually, with the mingled sound of rolling carriages, of heavy waggons, and the trampling of horses' feet. Magnificent equipages drive along the smoothly gravelled roads, with which the modern park that extends around the old tree is intersected.   Riders on steeds, such as the ancient Britons saw not, and even the polished Romans could hardly have imagined, pass and repass among the trees, and gaily attired pedestrians walk beneath their shade. Strange contrast to what has been ! The mental eye, back glancing through the vista of long ages, still loves to dwell on the loneliness and the grandeur, on the gloom and depth of the wide forest : it mourns over the ages and the generations that have passed away, since the memorial trees emerged from their cradle in the earth. Some hand might inscribe on their rough bark that all is vanity, that the glorious earth was not designed to be thus made a charnel-house; but, among those who pass the aged trees, few would stop their progress, or their discourse, to read the inscription; and, among those who read, fewer, perhaps, would desire that it should be otherwise.

Hatfield Oak.

Hatfield-Oak.

[Queen Elizabeth is said to have been seated beneath the shade of
Hatfield Oak when she received intelligence of the death of her
sister Mary.]

How dim and indistinct the silent scene!
  O'er groves and valleys sleeping mists are spread,
Like a soft silvery mantle; while the stream,
  Scarce heard to flow, steals on its pebbly bed;
Nor e'en a ripple wakes the silence round,
As if it flowed, perchance, through some enchanted
    ground.

But O, the gorgeous tint, the dazzling glow
  In the clear west; for scarce the sun is gone!
That glowing tint doth yet a radiance throw
  On the hill-top, while, aye, each old grey stone
Glitters like diamonds 'mid the mountain heath,
While fades, in deep'ning gloom, the sleeping vale
    beneath.

One lonely spot, which oft, in solemn mood,

  Men have gazed on in ages long gone by,

Where stands that relic of the good green wood,

  The aged oak, prompting a tear or sigh ;

That lonely spot gleams o'er the misty scene,

Catching the splendour of the dazzling sheen.

And, aye, the lichens that have fixed deep

  Their tiny roots within the furrowed bough ;

And one small flower, which still her vigils keep,

  The blue forget-me-not, are glowing now,

In characters, methinks, of living flame,

Seeming to print the old oak's massy frame.

It looks as if a bright and sudden beam,

  Within that oak, broke forth with fervid ray,

Tinting its old boughs with a golden gleam,

  Bright as the deep glow of the parting day ;

Tempting the passer-by to linger still,

Amid the deep'ning gloom that broods o'er dale and
    hill.

Ah ! linger still, nor fear the chill night-wind ;

  It comes not yet, for scarce the sun is gone !

Each living emblem, speaking to the mind,

  May counsel well, and cheer, if reft and lone,

Thy sad thoughts, earthward bend, giving but little heed

To signs of mercy near, waiting each hour of need.

Men may learn from them, be it joy or pain,
  That bids the heart its wonted calm forego,
Sunbeams, or showers, loud wind, or driving rain,
  The morning hoar frost, or the dazzling snow,
The small bird, journeying through the pathless skies,
May win dull thought, from earthly care to rise.

It might be, that in such a glowing hour,
  When shone the old oak, as with living flame,
While anxious thoughts within her breast had power,
  Forth from yon aged hall* a lady came
To meet the freshness of the evening breeze,
Viewless, yet rustling still among the trees.

Oh! there were hearts within that stately hall,
  Though ruined now, that beat with high alarm,
And champing steeds, and warders waiting all
  To guard, if need might be, from gathering harm,
And cautious looks, and voices speaking low,
As if they feared an hour of coming woe.

Yes, life or death, eternity or time,
  Waited the passing of that anxious day;
A throne, a prison, much perchance of crime,
  Should statesmen battle, each in stern array;
Should death steal onward through a palace gate,
Warning his victim from her hall of state.

---

* The Palace of Bishops Hatfield, then a royal residence, where
the Princess Elizabeth resided in a kind of honourable custody,
though still rigorously guarded.

The mind back glancing through long ages past,
   E'en to the changes in that fitful scene,
Calls forth from out the dim, the lone, the vast,
   One act to gaze on, noting what hath been
In dreamy life ; though all we now descry
Seems as a mournful vision sweeping by.

Look then on her, for whom no evening gleam,
   Nor soft wind rustling in the young green trees,
Can soothe the wasting grief—the fever'd dream—
   The wandering thought, finding but little ease ;
For each fond hope from the sad heart is flown,
Like leaves by autumn winds, all sear'd and gone.

Her hall is lonely now, her throne of state
   Strangers may gaze at ; one lone couch of pain
Holdeth her now, and pale care seems to wait
   Beside that couch, despite the weeping train
Who vainly seek, with fond officious zeal,
To soothe the rankling grief they may not heal.

Through the dim oriel streams that sunny glow
   Which tints the old oak with its parting beam
And one last flush gleams on the cold, damp
     brow
   Whence life is ebbing, like a fitful dream,—
Too soon for those whom anxious boding fill,
Her weeping train of ladies, watching still.

Why watch ye now ? Seven thunders would not wake
  That dreaded one—her load of life laid down.
Her sleep is sound.   Her stern heart may not ache,
  Nor throb the brow that wore a joyless crown;
An instant past a queen.   For love or hate,
She cares not now; waiting at mercy's gate.

Hark to swift footsteps on the dewy grass,
  'Mid the dim twilight, for the flush is gone
That lit yon death-couch.   Hasting on they pass
  To hail, as queen, the lone and captive one.
Captive, and yet a queen! one moment more
Shall give to her the crown that anxious Mary wore.

The Beech of the Frith Common.

The Beech of the Frith Common.

"Thrice fifty summers have I stood
In beauteous, leafy solitude,
Since childhood in my rustling bower
First spent its sweet and sportive hour,
Since youthful lovers in my shade
Their vows of truth and honour paid;
And on my trunk's smooth, glossy frame
Carv'd many a long-forgotten name:
Oh! by the vows of gentle sound,
First breath'd upon this sacred ground;
By all that truth hath whisper'd here,
Or beauty heard with willing ear,
As love's own altar honour me,
Spare, woodman, spare the beechen tree."—ROGERS.

LET him who loves to mark the changes of the seasons, and to watch the alternations which spring and summer, autumn and winter, produce in the vegetable kingdom, stand beside one of those magnificent columns which spring from out the parent earth, and bear on high a canopy of branches. Let him choose that season when the leaves are just beginning to expand, when the swelling buds assume a reddish tint, and here and there a young green leaf has unfolded, in all its freshness and its beauty, as yet unsoiled by a passing atom, or un-

beaten by a single rain-drop.   The clouds, how beautiful
they look, and the deep blue sky above them ! for both
are clearly seen through the ramified branches ; the first,
when driven swiftly by soft breezes from the west; the
other, in all its grandeur and extent, as when the morn-
ing stars rejoiced together, and it first appeared like a
glorious pavilion based on the distant hills.

Such is the Beech of the Frith Common.   It stands
alone in the centre of a beautiful common, covered with
wild flowers and short herbage, and the fragrant thyme,
among which the industrious bee loves to nestle, and to
gather in her harvests.   The nest of the skylark is
among the juniper-bushes that skirt the margin of the
common ; its joyous tenant is up in air, warbling and
rejoicing, and making his high home resound with
melody.   And well may he rejoice, for he has no
sadness to damp his song, no earth-born cares to bring
him down.   But if we seek for one, albeit assigned
to earth, and being unable to soar into mid air, yet
thankful and making the best of her humble lot, list
to the contented cuckoo ; she bids the valley ring with
her note, it is unvaried, and some people would fain say
that it is wearisome;—no such thing, it is the very voice
of spring, telling of sweet flowers and lengthening days,
of soft May showers, and of the coming of wandering
birds from far-off shores, to make glad the fields of
Britain.   The Beech of the Frith Common has no voice
with which to swell the chorus that has just begun, and

which increases daily, as first one musician and then
another, comes in aid. But this noble tree is to the
eye what music is to the ear. Look at the stately stem,
how smooth and glossy; time has not yet furrowed it,
nor has the pendent lichen and gray moss rooted them-
selves in its rough fissures. No records of human crime,
nor human care are chronicled upon its bark, no ruin
stands near on which the woes of ages have gathered and
brood heavy; no associations connected with the beautiful
tree, of midnight murders and broken hearts, the tears of
orphans and the prayers of oppressed ones, for patience or
for redress. Neither is there any trace upon the common,
that a circle of unhewn stones ever stood within its pre-
cincts, where unhallowed rites were practised, and midnight
incantations uttered; nor even that the grave of Briton
or of Gaul, of Roman or of Saxon, were made there,
for the turf is smooth as velvet.

Stately stands the tree, the tree beloved of all. The
oak is a majestic tree, the chesnut one of the most
umbrageous of forest trees, the elm rises like a pyramid
of verdure, the ash has its drooping branches, the
maple is celebrated for its light and quivering foliage, but
the beech is the poets' tree, the lovers' tree. Have you
not heard that young men often haunt the forest, and
disfigure the even and silvery bark of beech-trees,
by making them the depositors of the names of their
beloved ones ? " The bark," say they, " conveys a happy
emblem," and while thus employed they please them-

selves with thinking, that as the letters of the name
increase, so will their love.

Here then stands the beech-tree, in all its dignity and
fair proportions, its firm trunk based in the earth, but
with no knarled roots upheaving the soil around, and
making it unsightly.   When the celebrated Smeaton
pondered within himself concerning the possibility of
constructing a building on the Eddystone rock, which
might resist the tremendous violence of contending seas,
which had swept away the previous erections of Win-
stanley and Rudyerd, and left not a stone remaining ;
seas which dash at least two hundred feet above the
rock, and the sound of whose deafening surges resemble
the continuous roar of thunder, his thoughts involuntarily
turned towards the oak.   He considered its large
swelling base, which becomes reduced to one third,
occasionally to one half of its original dimensions,
by a gradual and upward tapering of the living shaft,
and it appeared to him that a building might be
erected on the model of the oak, that would be fully able
to resist the action of external violence.   Thus thinking,
he projected the light-house of Eddystone, which soon
proved, amid the tremendous fury of contending
elements, that he had not erred in taking nature for
his guide.   A beech or elm might have suggested the
same thought, for in the trunk of every forest-tree the
material is so disposed that the greater portion pertains
to the base of the column ; that part, especially, which

rises from the root is thickest, and why is this? not only because a tapering column is far more beautiful than one of equal girth, but because the disturbing force at the top, acts more powerfully on the lower sections, than on the higher. It is needful that the base of the column should be strengthened, and it is equally unnecessary that the top should be of the same thickness as the base. Two purposes are consequently answered. The tree is rendered stronger and more elegant, and a certain portion of material is given to one part, without weakening the other. A tree is, therefore, equally adapted by its construction to resist the fury of the tempest, of that unseen, yet mighty force which comes against it, when the fierce northern blast howls through the forest; as also the load of snow which often presses heavily upon its topmost branches.

There is not throughout the vegetable kingdom a more glorious object than a tree, with its smooth and tapering trunk, and its canopy of mingling boughs. Who can estimate correctly the majesty with which it is invested, or the grace and grandeur of its proportions, and its bulk? The finest trees often grow on mountainous heights, harmonizing with the illimitable expanse of heaven, or surrounded with the wildest extent of forest scenery. Their intrinsic bulk is therefore lessened to the eye, and it is not till they are singled from the surrounding landscape, and subjected to a rule and measure, that an opinion can be formed with respect to their vast

size and height. Even then, the certainty often fails to
impress the mind, for figures convey but an imperfect
conception of length and breadth, of height and girth.
Some more familiar illustrations are wanting to prove
that many a majestic tree, which is admired among its
sylvan brethren, as the proudest ornament of a park or
forest, is in reality an enormous mass, which the passer-
by would gaze at with awe and admiration, if seen
beside the dwellings and the palaces of men; or com-
pared with the moving objects which pass and repass in
the streets of a great city. Our native woods often con-
tain noble specimens, of which the bulk is ten or
twelve feet in diameter, a width greater by three feet
than the carriage-way of Fetter lane, near Temple-
bar; and oaks might be named, on the block of
which two men could thresh without incommoding one
the other. The famous Greendale Oak is pierced by a
road, over which it forms a triumphal arch, higher by
several inches than the poets' postern at Westminster
Abbey. The celebrated table in Dudley Castle which is
formed of a single oaken plank, is longer than the
wooden bridge that crosses the lake in the Regent's
park; and the roof of the great hall of Westminster,
which is spoken of with admiration on account of its
vast span, being unsupported by a single pillar, is little
more than one-third the width of the noble canopy of
waving branches that are upheld by the Worksop Oak.
The massive rafters of the spacious roof rest on strong

walls, but the branches of the tree spring from one common centre. Architects can alone estimate the excessive purchase which boughs, of at least one hundred and eighty-nine feet, must have on the trunk into which they are inserted. Those of the Oak of Ellerslie cover a Scotch acre of ground; and in the Three-shire Oak, its branches drip over an extent of seven hundred and seven square yards. The tree itself grows in a nook that is formed by the junction of the three counties of York, Nottingham, and Derby; and as the trunk is so constructed, being tapering and firmly rooted in the earth, in order that it may uphold the boughs and repel the fury of the winds, so are the boughs themselves, made with an especial reference to the purpose for which they are designed. They are much thicker at the place of their insertion in the trunk than at the extremity; that their tendency to break may thus be uniform. We owe to this, the graceful waving of innumerable boughs, here aspiring in airy lightness above the general mass, and there gracefully feathering to the ground, the pleasing murmur of their foliage when rustling in the warm breeze of summer, and the elegant ramifications which are perceptible in winter. But whether seen against the clear blue ether of a winter sky, or presenting a broad and ample breadth of shade; whether raged against by a fierce tempest, or having the foliage gently shaken by playful breezes; the giant resistance in one case, or the ceaseless quiver of the other, owe their power, and their play, to the unseen members of the mighty column which are buried deep within the earth. These, though still, are ever working. Though they cannot move themselves, they move others. They draw up the moisture of the earth and send it, by means of a secret influence on an undiscoverable machinery, which is seen in its effects, though the way in which it operates is entirely unknown, to fill with life the smallest leaf that quivers in the sunbeams, or the tender bud that is not yet emerged from its silken cradle.

They serve likewise to brace the tree within the earth, and they vary according to climate and locality. Take the beech for instance, which flourishes alike in deep valleys, and on windy hills. When growing in a sheltered place the roots are thrown out equally, like rays diverging from a common centre. When standing on an eminence or on a plain, exposed to the action of a wind that blows generally from one quarter, the roots spread out and grapple the firm soil towards the quarter from which the wind comes. In this country it is generally south-west, or west-south-west; hence it happens that when other causes do not interfere, our native trees generally incline their heads to the north-east, and their strongest roots go forth in an opposite direction, for the evident purpose of holding the tree firm, when the storms beat upon it. Trees are, consequently, often uprooted by a sudden squall of wind from the east or north-east, which have withstood the tempests of ages.

The aggregate effect produced by forest scenery is magnificent—the deep retiring woodland, the waving of innumerable branches, the majestic columns which uphold them, the mingled tints and hues, the dancing of the lights and shadows on the ground, the long, long vistas which extend far as the eye can reach, when the view of external nature is shut out, when there is neither a green meadow nor distant hill to be seen, nor even a fence nor railing, nothing which betokens the hand of man; but noble trees around, and a magnificent canopy of mingled boughs; when not a sound is heard except the rustling of the wind in the topmost branches, or perchance the plaintive voice of the ring-dove, which loves to build her nest in solitary places. But the tree, which like the Beech of the Frith Common, stands alone, can best be understood. The mind can rest upon it, and the eye can embrace its beautiful proportions. Wisdom may be gained by him who loves to read the ample page of nature, while musing beneath its branches, for every leaf is an open book, every tender bud tells much concerning the goodness of that Being whose beneficence is equally conspicuous in the smallest, as in the mightiest of created things.

> This noble tree grows on a sunny hill side,
>   And merry birds sing round it all the day long;
> Oh the joy of my childhood, at evening tide,
>   To sit in its shadow and list the birds' song!

No sound then was heard but the gush of the rill,
  Or the woodpecker tapping some hollow beech-tree;
While the sun shed his last purple glow on the hill,
  And the last hum was heard of the home-loving bee.

But now far away from that sunny hill side,
  'Mid the stir and the din of the proud city's throng,
I think, is that tree standing yet in its pride?
  Are the echoes still woke by the merry birds' song?

They tell me the woodcutter's hatchet was heard,
  To thin the tall trees where they drooped o'er the lea;
But he marr'd not the home of the wandering bird,
  The haunt of my childhood, my own beechen-tree.

May peace in the cot of that woodman abide,
  And grateful birds sing to him all the day long,
May his steps long be firm on the sunny hill's side,
  And echo respond to the voice of his song.

I can think of that tree, where no green trees are seen,
  'Mid the city's loud din, for the spirit is free,
And dear to me still is the wild daisied green,
  Where thy branches are waving, my own beechen-tree.

THE SALCEY OAK

The Salcey Oak.

———————

" Thou wert a bauble once, a cup and ball,
   Which babes might play with, and the thievish jay,
   Seeking her food, with ease might have purloin'd
   The auburn nut that held thee, swallowing down
   Thy yet close-folded latitude of boughs,
   And all thy embryo vastness at a gulph."—COWPER.

By virtue of those indices which naturalists discover in the trunks and boughs of aged trees, it is conjectured that the autumns of fifteen hundred years have visited the Oak of Salcey. Standing remote from those frequented parts of Britain, where a thronging population causes the increase of buildings and the making of new roads, protected also by the inland situation of the little forest by which it is surrounded, the old tree has remained entire. It stands a living cavern, with an arched entrance on either side, within whose ample circumference large animals may lie down at noon, and where the careful shepherd often folds his flock at nightfall. It measures forty-six feet ten inches at the base, and at one yard from the ground the girth is thirty-nine feet ten inches.

The knotted roots of the old tree have been laid bare by time or accidents, or by that living principle which causes aged trees to unearth their roots, and to raise the soil into hillocks; successive storms or the heavy tread of cattle have worn away the hillocks, and the roots being left in arches, produce an equally fantastic and picturesque effect. I have frequently observed the same peculiarity among the deep beech-woods of Gloucestershire; grass does not generally grow beneath them, yet in places open to the sun, primroses nestle in the interstices, and long pendent fern-leaves with the nailwort and forget-me-not grow profusely; but more commonly the bare and knarled roots are without verdure, and they often afford a welcome covert to the wild rabbit, who makes them the portals of her burrow.

The effect which is thus produced is well deserving the attention of the artist. The roots of such trees as grow on high and rugged banks, are occasionally unearthed to the extent of several feet, while between them, are deep hollows, running far back, with masses of freestone, and pendent ferns; and groups of innocent sheep, may be often seen with their heads projecting beneath the long fibres of the thickly tangled roots. Pliny relates that in countries subject to the shock of earthquakes, or where the living principle in trees is extremely vigorous, in consequence of soil or climate, the roots are often raised to a surprising height, that they look like arches, beneath which troops of cavalry may pass, as through the open and stately portals of a town.

The venerable tree which has given rise to this digression, stands in the centre of a grassy area, where cattle pasture, and though still bearing the name of forest, the site on which it grows, exhibits little that would recall to mind, that it was once covered with noble trees. A few still remain, some apparently of great age, others in different stages of growth or of decay; but to the eye and to the heart, the one which is called by pre-eminence the Salcey Oak, must be alone.

He who loves to watch the motions of animals, and the flight of birds; the passing of summer clouds, and the gradual advancing and receding of the light; the aspect too of nature, when shone upon by the bright warm sun-beams or at the fall of night, may find much to interest him in, and around the time-worn tree. Seen dimly in the dubious nights of the summer solstice, it presents the aspect of a cavern overgrown with bushes, within which a flock of sheep are often quietly reposing, or a cow has laid down to rest, with her little one beside her. The dew meanwhile is heavy on the grass, and not a sound is heard. The inmates of the nearest farm-house are not yet moving, neither is any animal abroad, nor have the early birds left the boughs on which they rest. That sound of waters which of all others is the loudest, when all else is still, which seems to gather strength when

the night is deepest, and often causes him who loiters in
the fields to think that he is listening to the congregated
roar of some far-off torrent, when perhaps only a little
streamlet is brawling among the trees; that solemn
sound is not heard here, for no running streams are
close at hand. Nothing then is heard in the silence of
this lone hour, but the rustle of the aspen-leaves, which
are never still, even in the hot nights of summer, when
not a breeze is felt, or the last whoop of the gray owl,
when she hastens to shelter herself in the cavernous old
tree, for that is her favourite abode. The nightingale
does not affect the Oak of Salcey, neither does the lark
love to raise his voice in the midst of the old trees,
where no young copses, covered with wild roses and
honeysuckles, invite him to place his nest among them.

When the day dawns, and objects become visible,
forth come the hare and rabbit from their shady coverts,
and joyous birds from the shelter of trees and bushes.
The early blackbird, nature's sweetest minstrel, sings
loudly that all may hear, and shaking off their slumbers
may be up and doing; his full strain of melody does
not always wait for the rising of the sun, he rather bids
him welcome on his first appearance. Heralded by his
clear voice, the chorus of singing birds commences.
The lark rises high in air, the thrush and throstle, the
linnet and the goldfinch pour forth such enchanting
notes, as man, with all his science, cannot imitate. The
rays of the bright sun shine into the hollow of the tree,

and rouse the innocent sheep which slept there, to pasture
on the fresh grass; the cattle too are moving, some from
the great oak, others from the coppice-wood, which is
seen at intervals among the trees. The business of the
farm now commences, and the labourers are abroad.
You may, perhaps, chance to see one of them pass this way,
in going to, or returning from the fields, either to gather
in the crops of hay, or corn, or to plough the land ac-
cording to the season of the year. But this is of rare
occurrence, few care to visit the old oak, and the pathway
does not lead across the area by which it is surrounded.

At noon day when the sun is high, how quiet is this
place ! The song-birds are silent, but the hum of
insects is at its height; they float up and down,
and seem to rest on the soft air, as if threading the
mazes of a dance, and then advancing and retreating
with a ceaseless buzz. But when the shadow of the tree
lengthens upon the grass, and the beams of the setting
sun tint its topmost boughs of a golden hue, first one
bird carols, and then another. Then also the breathing
of the oxen, and the brushing sound which they make
in cropping the damp grass, become audible. No one
listens to them at noon, but the deep silence which
begins to steal over the place, when twilight renders the
large objects alone visible, brings the slightest movement
to the ear. At length even such faint sounds are heard
no longer; the birds cease their songs, and when the
moonbeams shine into the cavern which time has formed

in the Oak of Salcey, it may be seen that both sheep and cattle have retired thither.

At one season of the year the oak is beat upon by heavy rain, and loud winds howl furiously around its aged head ; at another it is white with snow, or the hoar frost of winter settles on it. At length green leaves peep forth from among the fissures of the trunk and boughs, and the sapling trees are green also.

There is little else to record in connexion with this aged tree. Peasants may have sheltered their flocks for ages beneath its canopy of branches, when those branches were full of sap, and when stately trees stood round in all their greatness, where now only a grassy area meets the eye. But no ancient ruins are to be seen by him who climbs the trunk, nor yet the traces of any city which might have invited the aggressions of an enemy. We conjecture, therefore, that a forest, with breaks of lawn and thicket, and perhaps a common on which the peasant built his hut, and the homestead arose in peaceful times, might have extended round the oak of Salcey. The ground on which we tread presents sufficient indications that such has been the case. The millfoil-yarrow, the wild camomile, the gravel birdweed, and stonebasil, ancient tenants of the soil, which grow only in the purest air of heaven, on waste land and stony banks, are seen in company with the wild bluebell and the crested cowwheat, with which the mower filleth not his hand, nor he that bindeth sheaves his bosom.

Old Trees in Welbeck Park.

" There oft the Muse, what most delights her, sees
Long living galleries of aged trees ;
Bold sons of earth, that lift their arms so high,
As if once more they would invade the sky.
In such green palaces the first kings reign'd,
Slept in their shades, and angels entertain'd.

With such old counsellors they did advise,
And, by frequenting sacred groves, grew wise.
Free from the impediments of light and noise,
Man, thus retir'd, his noblest thoughts employs."—WALLER.

VALLEYS and cultivated fields, have each their charac-
teristics of richness or of loveliness, but they have
no beauty in comparison with that of woodland scenery.
The wild thyme and moss, the short-cropped herbage,
the tufts of fern and golden-blossomed gorse, that vary
the ground on which we tread; the solemn depth of the
lone forest, the noble groups of trees that diversify the
open spaces, and the clear streams that flow silently
through the deep soil, bordered with cowslips and wild
marigolds, have all, and each, their own peculiar attrac-
tions. Who has not been sensible when passing among
them of an hilarity of feeling, a delight, which he
has experienced nowhere else, which carries him onward
from one spot to another, now in the midst of trees,
and now again in the open space, as if he could
never weary? Then, the sweet fresh breezes of the
spring, how pure they are, sporting over the green herb-
age or among the trees. They are not infected with
sighs of human sorrow; they have not passed beside the
couch of dying men, or through the throng of a great city.
They are sporting now as they sported a thousand years
ago, among the branches of some of the old trees, which
still remain, relics of bygone days, memorials of what
has been. Those breezes are still the same, for the

circumambient fluid, which gives hilarity and freshness to
everything that lives and moves on the surface of the
earth, is not subjected to the unalterable law which seems
impressed on all beside.   Earthly things grow old, or
assume some new character.   Even the kindred element
of water evaporates, and is replenished by means of rain
or dew; the soil is blown away in dust, and renewed
again by the decay of vegetables.   Men cease from off
the earth; in one day their thoughts perish; cities which
they have erected, noble structures, destined to last for
ages, crumble silently, or else are overthrown by war or
earthquakes; but the air, though ever moving, neither
evaporates, nor is susceptible of change.   Thus, then,
whether in the character of a whirlwind, or of zephyr;
whether as a breeze of spring, or tempest from the north,
has it raged or sported in the branches of the stately tree,
which stands among its brethren of the forest, resembling
a noble column, surrounded by crowding houses.   It is
termed the Duke's Walking-Stick, but the hand that
would essay to move the shaft from out the place where
it has stood for ages, must be gifted with a power and a
spell, which even the wildest fancy has never yet assigned
to any being of mortal mould; not even to those giants
of fierce bearing, with whom she loves to people her land
of fiction.   The column stands alone, its smooth trunk is
branchless to a giddy height, and its topmost boughs are
higher than the roof of Westminster Abbey at its loftiest
elevation.   A tree, with which the branches of no other

tree can mingle, solitary in the midst of its sylvan brotherhood, having no communion in its stateliness, either with the oak, over which long ages have passed, or with the sapling of yesterday. Thoughts of home and kindred are blended with that other tree, to which the lovers of forest scenery make a pilgrimage—the seven Sisters, for such is the name of a contiguous tree, with several columns, which, upspringing from the same root, are seen to mingle their leaves and branches. The bird which confides her nest in spring to the sheltering boughs of the one, teaches her young to nestle among the opening leaves of the other; so closely are they entwined, that a squirrel would find it difficult to make his way between them. We know not why the cognomen which distinguishes this favourite tree was given, or the period of its greatest perfection, whether it arose from out the earth in Saxon or Norman times, or whether seven ladies of a Ducal family, sisters in birth and love, gave that fond name to the noble tree, because of its interwoven stems.

The Queen's Oak.

O Lady! on thy regal brow
The shades of death are gathered now!
What matter, if in queenly bower,
Was past of life thy fitful hour ?
In cloister gray, where meets at eve
The whispering winds that softly breathe ;
Or, if in leafy glen afar,
To some lone cot the guiding star
Of him, who turn'd with weary feet
Thy joyous answering smile to meet ?
What matter, if in hut or hall,
Was spread o'er thee the funeral pall ;
If mutes and banners waited round,
Or flowrets decked thy simple mound ?
If wrought on earth thy Maker's will,
No meddling fiend shall work thee ill :
O blest thy waiting-place shall be,
Till the grave shall set her captive free,
Through His dear might who came to bless
Man in his utter helplessness.—M. R.

WHAT see you in that old oak more than in any other tree, except that its trunk is white with age, and that gray lichens hang in tufts from out the interstices of the bark ? That tree, stranger, was a silent witness of scenes long past. It stood when England was rent

L

asunder during the fearful contest of the Roses; and beside its noble trunk met those, in all the pride of chivalry and loveliness of beauty, who now are resting from life's weary pilgrimage beneath the tomb of Quentin Matsys.

Who has not heard concerning the Duchess Dowager of Bedford, how she left her high estate to wed a simple squire, and to dwell with him in the beautiful solitude of her dower castle of Grafton, far from the scene of her former greatness! The noble trees that grouped around the castle wall, mingled with those of the wide forest of Whittlebury, a royal chase, on the verge of which, and at no great distance from the castle, stood this aged tree, then in all the pride of sylvan majesty; and far as the eye could reach, extended one vast sweep of woodland scenery, with breaks of lawn and thicket. The inhabitants of Grafton Castle passed the first years of their wedded life in comparative obscurity, exercising hospitality, according to the manners of the age, yet keeping as much as possible apart from the dangers and excitements of public life. At length the necessity of providing for the elder branches of an increasing family, rendered it desirable to strengthen their connexions, and the Duchess of Bedford, whose rank was more exalted than her fortune, resolved to introduce them at the court of her friend, Queen Margaret, to whom her eldest daughter, the beautiful Elizabeth Woodville, was appointed maid of honour.*

* Hall's Chronicle, p. 365. Parliamentary History. Vol. II. 345.

Years passed on, and Elizabeth was united to John Gray, son and heir to Lord Ferrars of Groby, possessor of the ancient domain of Bradgate,* by reason of his descent from Petronilla, daughter of Grantmesnil, one of the proudest of our Norman nobility. Withdrawn from her quiet home by the stirring incidents that attended the fierce contest between the rival houses of York and Lancaster, Elizabeth accompanied her husband during the campaign, and shared with him in many of its perils. It was even said that Queen Margaret persuaded her to visit king-making Warwick in his camp, under the pretence of requesting some little favour, for the stout earl was ever kind to her; but in reality to make observations relative to the number and condition of his troops. This was on the eve of the great battle of St. Albans, which took place at a short distance from the abbey. The abbey stood, in peaceable times, like a vast granary, which continually received and gave out its produce, into which was gathered both corn, and wine, and oil, barley, and the fruits of the earth, and to which not fewer than twelve cells and hospitals were appended. And scarcely was there a forest, chase, or wood throughout the greatest part of England, which did not in some measure contribute a supply to the abbey of its timber or venison. Successive monarchs banquetted within its walls, and while the abbots were distinguished for their extensive hospitality, the poor were not forgotten. Thus stood St. Albans,

* Afterwards the home of Lady Jane Gray.

often in stormy times a place of refuge, into which the
peasants drove their cattle and were secure, and while the
storm of war raged furiously without, there was safety and
abundance within. But it was not always so, and St. Albans
was sacked more than once. The infuriated followers of
Wat Tyler set fire to the papers and written records of the
abbey, and in after times it was exposed to all the horrors
of civil war, when the rival houses of York and Lancaster
battled close beside its walls, and beneath the floor of our
Lady's chapel rest the remains of many who fought and
fell in those murderous conflicts. Showers and warm
sunbeams contribute their aid ofttimes to repair the
ravages which war has made in the aspect of nature.
The trodden fields were again covered with corn; dwell-
ings which had been set on fire, were speedily rebuilt,
and all went on as before. Tributes of corn, and wine,
and oil, were brought into the abbey, and the poor
and destitute received their daily doles. But men had
not yet learned that war and misery are synonymous.
The second battle of St. Albans, at which the forces of
Queen Margaret were, for a brief space, triumphant, was
deeply felt within the abbey. Wounded men, borne by
their companions from the fray, were continually brought
in; and when the battle ceased, it was fearful to hear the
continual tolling of the bell, sounding daily from morn-
ing till night, while the dead were being interred ; if
holding rank among the living, within the precincts of the
monastery, if otherwise, in an adjoining field.*   The hus-

* History of St. Albans.

band of Elizabeth Woodville, Gray Lord Ferrars, was then in the twenty-fifth year of his age. Handsome, valorous, and intrepid, and devotedly attached to the cause of Henry VI.; he was appointed commander of the Red-rose cavalry, and, while leading on the memorable onset by which the field was won, he received a mortal wound, of which he died a few days after, at the village of Colney, on the twenty-eighth of February 1461.* Henry VI. visited and endeavoured to console the dying youth, and sought, with the usual kindliness of his nature, to reconcile him to the thought of death, by pointing to the only Refuge, on whom his own hopes rested. Some chroniclers relate, that, according to the fashion of the age, he conferred the honour of knighthood on the wounded earl, for the sake of his sons, for although his father, Lord Ferrars, had died two months before, the distracted condition of the country had prevented the young nobleman from taking his place in the house of peers. A deep and rancorous feeling seems to have existed against the memory of this brave and devoted adherent of King Henry; his harmless children, the eldest of whom was not more than four years of age, were deprived of their inheritance, and his widow was not permitted to remain on the family estate; the fine old mansion, with its broad lands, was confiscated; it became the property of another, who repaired thither to take possession, and with him his family and dependents, who filled all the offices and

* Whethemstede and Guthrie.

places of trust and profit which the adherents of the house
of Gray had hitherto enjoyed. Elizabeth, therefore, sought
again the paternal roof. Sad was the day of her return,
yet she only was changed. The avenue of noble trees
waved in the breeze, fresh and shady as when last she
passed ; the fields, too, looked as green and lovely, and
through them lay the pathway, fringed with wild flowers,
where she had often gathered, with her young companions,
fresh garlands of sweet flowers, with which to bedeck them-
selves. The mansion had not been altered, since the
family returned from court, at the accession of Edward
IV. There was the open door, down the steps of which
the train of sisters had followed their stately mother, when
they set forth a few years before, at the invitation of
Queen Margaret, to visit her court; the eldest, appointed
to be her maid of honour; * the others, with promises of
favour and promotion. They had now returned, for
there was neither favour nor promotion for adherents of
the Red-rose, and Catherine, and Anne, and Mary, were
waiting to receive Elizabeth with blended feelings of joy
and sorrow ; joy, to welcome back their sister ; sorrow,
to see her widow's weeds and orphan children. Time
had not changed them, nor were the faithful servants,
who had seen, a few years back, their young mistress
depart, with tears and blessings, yet broken down.
Here, then, at a short distance from this time-worn
tree, Elizabeth continued to reside in Grafton Castle,

* Parliamentary History. Vol. II. p. 345.

devoted to the education of her sons; for whom, as well as for herself, she was dependent on the bounty of her father.

Edward came at length to hunt in the forest of Whittlebury, for this great forest was a royal chase, abounding with shady coverts and open spaces, where the fern grew wild and high, and dancing lights and shadows seemed to sport over a wilderness of broken ground and coppice-wood. Elizabeth heard that he would pass at a short distance from her mother's dower castle, and she resolved to wait for him under the shade of the tall tree, which bears her name. The mingled sound of hounds and horns, with the trampling of horses on the green turf, soon reached her ear, and presently the monarch passed that way with his gallant train of hunters. She was then, for such is the tradition of the neighbourhood,* with her fatherless boys, on this very spot, for she had thrown herself on the ground, and besought him, with many tears, to have pity on her impoverished and bereaved children. The sight of beauty in affliction softened the stern heart of the monarch, while the anxiety of a mother for her children seemed to awaken in his heart feelings of kindliness and compassion, to which he had been long a stranger, and he raised her from the ground, with assurances of favour and consideration.

Legends tell, that they met again under the same old

* Baker's Northamptonshire.

tree, for that Edward seemed to prefer that their inter-
views should take place where he had first seen and loved
the beautiful Elizabeth. History relates that the espousals
were privately solemnised early in the morning of the
first of May 1464, at the town of Grafton, near Stony
Stratford. None were present excepting the Duchess of
Bedford, the priest, and two gentlewomen, with a young
man, who assisted in singing. The priest who wedded
them lies buried before the altar, in the church of the
Minoresses at London-bridge.*

> O what a mingled throng are passing now,
> As in a mirror, which time seems to hold
> For men to gaze in ! Actors in all scenes,
> Mingled, and yet distinct, with names on each,
> Given by Him who sent them forth to bless
> Their homes or kindred—dwelling where they may.
> Kings, with their crowned heads, and he who serves—
> The anxious tradesman, and the gentle one
> Who walks with peace, looking on meads and streams—
> Loving the sound of whispering winds at eve,
> Of warbling birds, and prattling streams that gush
> 'Mid flowers and ferns, and green hills meeting round ;
> For such are seen, e'en near the deadly fray
> Of battle fields, where meet the sire and son.
> The Red-rose conquering now—and then the Pale ;
> And he, who skulks in forest haunt, or cave
> When morning dawns, walks as a chief at eve.

Look, then, at the strange eventful scenes in the life
of Elizabeth Woodville, as they pass before the mental

* Fragment Chronicle, printed by Heane, at the end of the Sprott.
Chronicle.

vision, now in brightness and in beauty, and now in shade
and sadness.

Observe that gallant gentleman, holding a lady by the
hand, in a large and antique apartment, for the scene has
changed from Grafton Castle to the old palace of Reading.
That gentleman is Edward IV., and standing round, are
peers and princes of the realm, adherents of the house of
York, whom the king has convened in council, that he
may present to them the lady Elizabeth as his rightful
queen,—one whom he had wedded because of her
exalted worth, for he could never hope to espouse a
foreign princess, on account of the house of Lancaster.*
The queen is apparently little more than twenty-eight
years of age, and her delicate and modest beauty is not
impaired by either time or sorrow.   Her head is encircled
with a high crown of peculiar richness, the numerous
points of which are finished by fleur-de-lis.   Rich pearls,
strung in an elaborate pattern, encircle her beautiful
neck, while a small ring, in the middle of her forehead,
divides her pale yellow tresses, which descend in waving curls
of great length and profusion.   Her face is exceedingly
fair, and her eyes are timidly cast down.   She is royally
attired in a splendid kind of gold brocade, woven in
stripes of blue and gold, of which the wearing is restricted
to the royal reigning family, with a close boddice and tight
sleeves, and ermine robings, turned back over the shoul-
ders, and the whole dress is girded round the waist with

* The Sprott. Chronicle.

a crimson scarf. Her skirt is full and flowing, with a broad ermine border, and a train of many yards in length, held up by a trainbearer, a fair and gentle-looking damsel, most probably one of the queen's sisters, who has gracefully folded the extremity around her arms. A rich blue satin petticoat is seen beneath the drapery, and the shoes that peep forth occasionally are of a pointed form.*

From that old room of state, where stands the fair young queen, thus regally attired, passes on the pageant of king and lady, and bearded counsellors, in solemn pomp, to the stately abbey church of Reading, the lady led by the young Duke of Clarence, where she is publicly declared queen; and where having made her offering, she is receiving the congratulations of the assembled nobility, among whom, some people say, is the Earl of Warwick. Brilliant fêtes and tournaments succeed, such as have not been seen in England, since the gorgeous days of Edward III., when he held high state in Windsor Castle. Elizabeth presides in all, with her lovely train of sisters, and around them gather, as shepherds to " the star of Arcady, or Tyrian cynosure," many a gallant knight and noble, proud to tilt in honour of those fair damsels, and to receive from them the prize that beauty awards to valour. Listen now to the loud hum that mighty London sends through all her gates, for sights and sounds of revelry pertain to this bright act in the

* Lives of the Queens of England, by Alice Strickland.

life of our sovereign lady.   Knights, and citizens, and
throngs of people are filling every street, and crowding
every window.   The queen is passing through the city
to her palace of Westminster, in a litter borne on poles,
and supported by stately prancing steeds; and right and
left, behind and in advance, ride valiant men, whom
the king has deputed to this honour.   The queen has
come from Eltham Palace, where the hawthorn-trees are
all in blossom, and the little birds are singing blithely,
as if to hail their queen on the day of her corona-
tion.   And when the train of knights and citizens is
seen passing beneath the lofty portal of the ancient
abbey, sweet sounds greet them, not of joyous birds
that warble their harmonious concerts among the
trees in Eltham park, but deep solemn music, and
glorious human voices chanting in unison ; and thus
welcomed and attended, enters Elizabeth, to pass
forth again a crowned and anointed women.   And with
her is Count James, of St. Pol, uncle to the Duchess of
Bedford, with a hundred knights and their attendants ;
a sovereign prince, and near kinsman of the queen,
whom Charles the Bold had deputed to be present at
the coronation.   King Edward desired that the peers of
England and the citizens of London should be assured
that the lady whom he married was worthy, by her high
descent, to share his throne, and he had requested the
French king to induce some of the princes of the house
of Luxemburg to visit England, and claim kindred with

his wife. Count James set forth accordingly, for now that his fair cousin wore a crown, he was proud to acknowledge the connexion. It was otherwise a few years before with the house of Luxemburg : they had not only chosen to forget the mother of Elizabeth, because she married a private gentleman, " though he was the handsomest man in all England, and the duchess was an exceeding handsome gentlewoman." They had not only chosen to withold their countenance, but had even spoken such harsh words, that neither the knight nor lady dared to claim kindred with them on the continent, for the father of that same count, who was now in England, would have slain them both, had they ventured within his reach. All was now forgotten, and he who looks with the mental eye through the long, long vista of past ages, may discern in the dim distance, gorgeous pageants, and tilts and tournaments, ladies coming forth from their old Gothic castles to grace the court, with chevaliers of France and England, each from their baronial residences, mingling in feats of arms and festivals. And then, beside the small couch of a fair infant, are seen standing the haughty Cicely of York, and the royally descended Jaquetta of Bedford, grandmothers of the young scion, made friends that day, as they bend with looks of love over the unconscious sleeping one. Sleep on, fair child, thy brow shall wear a crown, but weary years of woes and wanderings are before thee.*

* Monstrelet.

The hand of the reaper,
    Cuts the ears that are hoary:
But the voice of the weeper,
    Wails manhood in glory. —SCOTT.

It is the middle of corn harvest, and reapers are cutting down the rich brown ears, on the verge of the great forest, where first met the Lady Elizabeth and King Edward. All around the Queen's Oak, the oak of Whittlebury Chase, is one vast joyous solitude of woods and waters, lonely, yet cheerful; without any habitation, yet not unpeopled, for noble antlers are seen emerging from the brushwood, and joyous birds and butterflies fly in and out among the trees, or flit from one flower to another. All is stillness, and beauty, and luxuriance; and let him who has found a covert within the woody range, venture not far away, for there are fearful doings in the land.

Gradually melt away the mists of time, that have hidden for a while the court of Westminster, but the king is not there, nor yet the queen, nor the couch on which the young child lay; but instead of these, strange men are seen hurrying from room to room, as if in quest of plunder. The moon is up, and her pale beams shine on the white sails of a small vessel, that urges its way, as in fear, from the shores of Lynn, in Norfolk.*
They shine, likewise, on a mother with three little girls, and a noble looking dame, the Lady Scrope, who have taken refuge in a strong and gloomy building at the end of St.

* Hall. Comines.

Margaret's church-yard. That lone mother is the beautiful Queen of England, she has fled to sanctuary on the approach of Warwick's army, for the ship, whose white sails glisten in the clear cold moonbeams, conveys her husband abroad in quest of succour. Stern men are prowling round the gloomy building, but no one dares to go within, for the queen has registered herself and her three children, Elizabeth, Mary, and Cicely, and the Lady Scrope, as inmates of sanctuary. That gloomy place has sheltered murderers and robbers, men, too, who were in peril of their lives, for treason against their king; but in the present evil times, ladies and young children often find a home within its walls, when all other homes are broken up. And thus, all comfortless and forlorn, is waiting the Queen of England, for the birth of that fair child, who first saw light within the sanctuary of Westminster.* No distinction is there between the kindred of a prince or peasant, when the crown is put aside, no royal spell with which to chace away either want or sorrow. The Queen of England soon began to be in need, and must have been constrained to surrender to the army of Queen Margaret, had not provisions been secretly conveyed to her by a kind-hearted butcher of the name of Gould, who could not bear, he said, to think that the lady and her children should be distressed for lack of food.

* It is conjectured that the prince was born in the Jerusalem Chamber, which the kind abbot relinquished to the queen.

The infant prince is about to be baptized, and this
with no greater ceremony than if he had been a poor
man's child. A poor man's child might have more to
gladden him, smiling faces and fresh air, but around this
son of a throneless monarch are sad countenances and
gloomy walls.   No costly gifts are presented, and for
attendants there remain but one or two kind friends,
faithful among faithless thousands.   No cloth of gold
adorns the Gothic font of hewn stone, round which the
little band of fond and faithful friends are gathered,
while the sacred ceremony is performed by the sub-prior,
who gives to the young prince the name of his father.
Those who promise for him, poor child, that he shall re-
nounce the pomps and pleasures of the world, when his
noble patrimony seems lost to him, are his grandmother
and the Lady Scrope, that devoted woman, who adheres to
the queen in all her trials.   The good abbot, Thomas Mil-
ling, performs the office of godfather, no other man being
either willing or at hand to do the desolate one that service.

Hark now to the sound of cheerful voices.   They come
from those who no longer fear to be regarded as
adherents of the house of York.   King Edward is
returned, and with him a gallant company of gentlemen
are seen pressing onward to the sanctuary.   One mo-
ment more, the bolted doors fly open, and the king and
queen, with their three little girls, are preparing to leave
the sanctuary ; the infant prince, borne in the arms of
his nurse, and his blithe and gladsome sisters, making

the old walls resound with their joyous voices.　Men
speak much concerning the valorous conduct of Queen
Margaret, and all which she has done and suffered in
order to replace her husband on the throne.　But they
speak more of the gentle Elizabeth; how she had sat
down in meekness and in patience within the walls of
that dismal place, where murderers and traitors had har-
boured in other times, waiting quietly till it pleased the
Most High to send her better days, sojourning, indeed,
in trouble, heaviness, and sorrow, yet sustaining it as
became a Christian woman, having much to fear, yet
hoping against hope.*

The queen is playing now with her ladies at a courtly
game called the marteaux, while others are amusing
themselves as best befit them, according to the fashion of
the times.　King Edward is dancing with the Lady
Elizabeth, his eldest daughter, and all is mirth and
revelry, and joyousness, and well may those rejoice, who
but a few days before knew not where to find a hiding-
place.　Who is that stately gentleman, whose dress and
accent bespeak him from foreign parts, on whom all
eyes are turned, and even the king salutes with more
than kingly courtesy?　The Lord of Grauthuse, Louis
of Bruges.　At once a nobleman, a merchant, and a
man of letters, acting as deputy in the Low Countries
for his master, Charles the Bold.　He received and
welcomed his royal guest, when in the preceding year the

* Fleetwood's Chronicle.

king fled from Enlgand, with a few attendants, "the most distressed company of creatures that were ever seen, for Edward had left his military coat, lined with martin's fur, with the master of the ship, having no other means of paying him, and was put on shore in his waistcoat. Unlike many in those days, who made the exiles of either faction, whether of the red or paler rose, pay dearly for their prison-houses, or hard fare, the Lord of Grauthuse fed and clothed the king and his attendants. He lent him ships and money, without which he could not have returned to his family, and afforded him every facility for making good his landing on the shores of Britain.* The minstrel has ceased now, and night and silence pervade the castle. The moon, which looked down on the white sail of King Edward, passing in its swiftness and its loneliness over the dark waters, shines now on the ancient turrets of Windsor Castle, wherein the king is sleeping. And there, too, his wife and children, his courtiers and his guards, are resting, and no sound is heard except the heavy tramp of the warders as they go their rounds, or perchance the deep bay of some listening hound, which the leveret's light step on the damp grass has roused from his slumber.

Morning returns, and the cheerful sights and sounds of busy life. St. George's Chapel, with its painted windows and knights' banners are brightening in the

* Narrative of Louis of Bruges, Lord Grauthuse, edited by Sir F. Madden.

sunbeams, while our lady's mass is sung, with the full harmony of the choristers' sweet voices. The king is there, Lady Elizabeth and the Lord Grauthuse, for it seems as if his late deliverance from so much peril had wrought good thoughts within him.

Again the scene is changed, from the chapel to the quadrant. The innocent young prince is being carried by Sir Richard Vaughan. He can hardly speak as yet, but his chamberlain has taught him to bid the Lord Grauthuse welcome, who saved his father, and brought himself from his dolorous birth-place, to enjoy at once his liberty, and the sun's cheering light. That faithful chamberlain who carries the young prince everywhere, after his father's footsteps, will yet be called upon to act in a very different scene. He is attending the king and count from place to place, now in the lodge at Windsor Park, where the royal family dine together, afterwards through the garden and vineyard of pleasure, for the king desires to show his guest the many and varied excellencies of his kingly dwelling.

Pageants sweep by, and nobles are presiding in halls of state. See the monarch, too, in his kingly robes, with his cap of maintenance, and right and left his lords, both spiritual and temporal. And list to that grave man, who declares before the king and nobles, the intent and the desire of the commons, with regard to the queen and Lord Grauthuse; upon the one is bestowed all honour and commendation of her womanly behaviour and great con-

stancy during the nation's peril; to the other, is conveyed
that nation's gratitude for his kindness and humanity to
her sovereign lord, by the king, creating him Earl of
Winchester. And surely the ceremony of that creation
is one of no ordinary interest. The king is passing now
into Whitehall, and thither too goes the queen from her
own apartment, wearing a crown upon her head, with
the young prince in his small robes of state, borne after
her in the arms of Master Vaughan. And thus the
king and queen, and that fair child, proceed through
the abbey church, to the shrine of St. Edward, where
their offerings are presented. Next, in the review of
pageantries and banquet-halls, hunting scenes and revels,
in the beautiful bowers of Eltham Palace, rises from out
the mingled scene, the rich and gorgeous spectacle of the
betrothing of the young Duke of York with Anne Mowbray,
the infant heiress of the duchy of Norfolk. St. Stephen's
chapel is being hung with arras of gold, and men are
employed both day and night in putting up the drapery,
which standing in its richness, must yet be gracefully
arranged in broad folds around the pillars and the
columns. All this is done, and the closed doors are
opened for the entrance of stately ladies and train-
bearers, great lords and their attendants, the beauty and
the chivalry of the house of York. And now the flourish
of loud trumpets and the clang of cymbals announce
the king's approach, and the full quire is pealing forth
its melody of mingled voices and high minstrelsy. The

king is entering with the young Prince of Wales and the three princesses, Elizabeth, Mary, and Cicely; the queen follows, leading the small bridegroom of five years' old, her brother, Earl Rivers, conducts the baby bride, who looks awestruck and wondering, at the unusual sights and sounds. Thus striking its roots deep, with young scions rising round, stands the red rose of England in all its richness and luxuriance.

Look at that desolate woman, who is sitting all sorrowful and dismayed on the rushes that strew the floor of a large and antique apartment. Her long hair, once her richest ornament, has fallen from beneath her widow's cap, and flowing in all its wonted beauty, over her slight form, is resting on the pavement. Fearful scenes have passed before the view of England's queen since her proud day in St. Stephen's chapel—her husband's couch of death, his deep remorse for sins committed or duties passed over ; his funeral, his empty throne, murder, and usurpation. There is the sound of many footsteps treading heavily and in haste, and the putting down of boxes ; men are seen busy in conveying household stuff, and chests and packages, but that desolate woman does not seem to heed them—she is thinking only of her sorrows, and the dangers that surround her family, for intelligence was brought to her at midnight that the Duke of Gloucester had intercepted the young king on his way from Ludlow to the metropolis ; that he had seized his person, and caused the arrest of her brother, Earl Rivers, and Lord Gray, her son, together with the faithful Vaughan, who used to carry prince Edward when an infant.[*]

Bitterly does she lament having listened to the evil counsellors, who prevented her from placing a strong escort around the person of her son; but she remembered, even in the midst of her exceeding grief, that herself and her young family had before been saved by taking refuge in the sanctuary, and she resolved to go thither without delay. Rising up, therefore, in the midst of the dark night, she caused her innocent children to be brought to her, and hastened with them from the palace of Westminster to the residence of the good abbot. She knew that if able to keep her second son in safety, it would ensure the life of the young king; but she did not go as heretofore into the ancient sanctuary, for the whole of the abbey, with its rooms of state and spacious gardens, was equally privileged, and she felt that she was welcome. Never yet has the right of sanctuary been violated, even in the worst of times; and, perhaps, a ray of hope is lighting up in the breast of that lone woman; but now the door is opening, and the venerable Archbishop Rotherham, who resides in York-place, beside the abbey, enters, with a cheerful countenance, and communicates a message, sent him by Lord Hastings in the night, and which he believed to be of good import. Bourchier, the primate, accompanies him, and they come in full credence of the duke's good faith, who has endeavoured, with

[*] Cont. Hist Croyl. Sir Thomas More. Hall.

much sophistry, to convince the privy council that his designs are just and honourable.

The queen seems unwilling to receive their message ; her just apprehensions are not to be removed by the hopes which they endeavour to excite. The good archbishop seeks to comfort her by saying that he trusts the matter is none so sore as she takes it for, and that he is in good hope, and relieved from fear by the message sent from the Lord Chamberlain Hastings. " Ah, woe worth him," replies the queen, " for he is one of them that labours to destroy me and my children." "Madam," rejoins the bishop, " be of good cheer : I do assure you, if they crown any other king than your son, whom they now have with them, we shall, on the morrow, crown his brother, whom you have with you. And here is the great seal, which, in likewise, as that noble prince, your husband, delivered unto me, so here I deliver it unto you, to the use and behoof of your son.*

This sad scene, like others of joy and sorrow in the life of poor Elizabeth, is fading from before the view, but, while it lingers, look well at the spacious hall wherein the queen has taken refuge, with its circular hearthstone in the centre, and an opening in the roof above, through which the smoke escapes in winter. The further end is nobly screened with oak panelling, laticed at the top, and having several doors of ancient workmanship, that open on winding stairs, leading to numerous small stone cham-

* Sir Thomas More.

bers, with carved windows and stone mullions.   There
are also state apartments, of which the walls are covered
with richly carved oak ; an organ-room, and the abbot's
grand reception-room, with its Gothic window of painted
glass, but with such we have no concern.

May, sweet May is come, and the hearth-stone is
decked with green branches and bright flowers; the birth
of the young day, but withering before its close.
Emblems of the failing hopes of her who sits all desolate
beside them, and with her are two beautiful and serious-
looking maidens, the princesses Elizabeth and Mary,
and four young children, from three to eleven years of
age; Richard, Duke of York, Anne, Catherine, and
Bridget.   At one time the terrified children hide in the
folds of their mother's robe; at another, their cheerful
voices are heard, calling to each other as they run from
room to room; now in the state apartment, and now in
some winding passage, or asking leave to wander forth
among the bees and flowers in the quiet garden of the
abbey.   Poor children, your grief is light, and it passes
soon, like an April shower; bur darker clouds are gather-
ing, and their crushing rain will fall heavily even upon you.

An aged man is seen advancing towards the abbey, and
with him a deputation, apparently of no mean rank.   His
robes and crosier denote his dignity, for it is the Arch-
bishop of Canterbury, who is about to pay a visit to the
queen, with a message from the Lord Protector, who has
placed the young king in the Tower, under the pretence

of awaiting his coronation, and who also desires to gain possession of his brother. A long and stormy debate had taken place in the star-chamber, close to Elizabeth's retreat. It was argued there, that men and women might remain in sanctuary, but that young children had no need, they being guileless of all crimes that might affect the state ; that consequently the Duke of Gloucester might possess himself of his nephew whenever it pleased him. The archbishop was extremely concerned when he heard all this, and he proferred his services to speak with the queen, rather than force should be used.*

The scene has changed from the great hall, with its fresh flowers around the hearthstone, and its floor strewed with green rushes, to the great Jerusalem chamber, with its Gothic window of richly stained and painted glass, its curious tapestry, and ancient picture of King Richard. Observe the venerable man, beneath the surface of whose placid and pale features deep feelings are at work. He knows not what to say, nor how to prepare the mind of the poor queen for the stern resolve of the hunchbacked protector, with regard to the young prince. At length he began by urging that the king required the company of his brother, being much cast down for the want of a playfellow.

" Troweth the protector," replies the queen, (heaven grant that he may prove a protector,) " that the king doth lack a playfellow ? Can none be found to play

* Hall.

with the king but only his brother, who hath no wish to
play because of sickness ? as though princes so young as
they be, could not play without their peers, or children
could not play without their kindred, with whom, for the
most part, they agree worse than with strangers !" The
archbishop knew not what to say in answer, he liked not
to tell her that the protector was resolved to gain posses-
sion of the young prince, and he waited in the hope that
she might be inclined to accede to his request. At length
the queen, taking her son by the hand, said, in a com-
pressed and solemn tone, "My lord, and all my lords
now present, I will not be so suspicious as to mistrust
your truth. Lo here is this gentleman whom, I doubt not,
would be safely kept by me if I were permitted; and
well do I know there be some such deadly enemies to my
blood, that if they wist where any lay, they would let it
out if they could. The desire of a kingdom knoweth
no kindred ; brothers have been brothers' bane, and may
the nephews be sure of the uncle ? Each of these chil-
dren are safe while they be asunder; notwithstanding, I
here deliver him, and his brother's life with him, into
your hands, and of you I shall require them before God
and man. Faithful ye be, I wot well, and power ye
have, if ye list, to keep them safe; but if ye think I fear
too much, yet beware ye fear not too little ! Farewell, my
own sweet son ! God send you good keeping. Let me
kiss you once ere you go, for God knoweth when we shall
kiss together again." Tenderly embracing the afflicted

M

boy, she is seen "weeping bitterly over him, and he too is weeping as fast in his turn."*

Fearful tragedies are acting now in the dim distance of time's perspective. They flit before the mental view, fading, and seeming to appear again; yet not the same, though like in terror and in kind. The shadowy figures of Hastings, of Gray, and Rivers, are seen passing from the block, and then the innocent forms of two young children, emerging from the gloomy range of fortresses belonging to the Tower. And loud is heard the sobbing, and the pitiful screams of the poor mother, as she beats upon her breast, and calls her sweet babes by name; and, kneeling down, implores the vengeance of the Just One, on the guilty head of him who has thus cruelly deprived her of her sons.

The vaulted door of a spacious room is opening, and across the furthest end seems flitting a strange succession of sad scenes—a young child's † funeral passes, and then a burst of anguish comes remotely to the ear, as if across wide waters, from a stern man, who yet cannot hide his sorrow; then a woman's wail, but the wail soon dies away, and a death scene and a funeral pass in faint review. ‡ Then the great fight of Bosworth, where a king is slain, and another takes his crown; a bridal follows and a coronation.

Thus they pass; events of other days are shadows now;

* Hall, 355. Sir Thomas Moore, 358. † Only son of Richard
III. ‡ Death and funeral of Richard's Queen.

terrible, indeed, at the period of their reality, but when ended, how soon forgotten! yet not forgotten by the aged woman, who is resting, as in a quiet home, within that spacious room in the Abbey of Bermondsey. It is her right to be there, for the prior and monks are bound by their charter to entertain, and that most hospitably, the representative of their great founder, Clare, Earl of Glou-cester. Edward VI. was the sole heir of that family, and the queen dowager is privileged to occupy the nobly panelled halls, and state-chambers, that are expressly reserved for the descendants of the founder.*

The waves and billows of life's deepest waters have passed over that aged woman who is sitting in a richly carved chair, at the great oriel-window, watching the summer clouds as they flit over the smiling landscape, and cast their shadows on the abbey fields. Her venerable figure, beautiful even in its decrepitude, though not with the beauty of sunny youth, yet such as the bright ray of the setting sun sheds over an autumn landscape, recalls the faint remembrance of a lovely woman who once stood, with two orphan boys beneath the oak of Whittlebury, to sue for the restitution of her broad lands, from the gallant Edward.

Hark to the toll of the convent bell. It is tolling for Elizabeth Woodville, late Queen Dowager of Eng-land, and the requiem is being sung, which breathes peace to the passing spirit. The moon is up, and yet the

* Annals of the Abbey of Bermondsey.

night is dark and gloomy, by reason of the heavy clouds
that are rolling past, and he who looks narrowly on the
deep dark waters of the river may discern a small boat
gliding on, with the coffin of the queen on board, and
four attendants, but when the moon shines out you can
distinguish the prior of the Charterhouse by his robes,
with two others in deep mourning, yet without insignia,
by which to designate them, and one female figure. Now
the rowers stop, and the coffin is being carried through
the little park into Windsor Castle, a few torches serving to
guide the bearers, which appear and disappear among
the trees, like the twinkling lights of glow-worms in the
grass.

Stately figures are kneeling round the coffin, where it
remains for a while, ready to be borne to its last resting-
place, and among the mourners one is discerned in the
dress of a nun. Again the coffin is upborne, and the queen's
daughters fall behind, with a train of shadowy forms,
ladies, and earls, and viscounts, moving onward to St.
George's chapel. Strange it seems, that neither plumes
nor scutcheons are to be seen; that when the dirge
is being sung, the twelve old men, whose office it is
to chant the requiem for the dead, are not even clad in
sable vestments: appearing rather like a dozen old men
indiscriminately and hastily brought together for the
purpose, and permitted to retain the garments of poverty,
in which they were found, and, instead of flambeaux, they
light on the funeral with old torches and torches

ends.*   Some say, that the queen, when dying, expressed an earnest wish for a speedy and private funeral. If so, her request was punctually fulfilled. Yet still it is remarkable that no more of pomp should appertain to the obsequies of her who had been Queen of England—that scutcheons and nodding plumes, and other mourning tokens, were wanting to distinguish that illustrious one's last sojourn on earth.

* Arundel MSS. 30. referred to in the Lives of the Queens of England.

THE END.

Joseph Rickerby, Printer, Sherbourn Lane.

WORKS BY THE SAME AUTHOR.

PROGRESS OF CREATION,

CONSIDERED WITH REFERENCE TO THE PRESENT CONDITION OF THE EARTH.

"The Progress of Creation is among the luxuries of the age."— *British Magazine.*

"This very handsome and beautifully illustrated volume, shows not only that the writer has read much, but that she can touchingly and elegantly bring home to the heart the result of her moral and religious lessons."—*Monthly Review.*

"We have no hesitation in recommending the Progress of Creation, as eminently calculated to exalt the mind and purify the heart."—*Scot's Times.*

"The plan of the work is original, the matter interesting and instructive."—*Atlas.*

"We have seldom met with a work, in which instruction and entertainment are more happily blended."—*Times.*

"This beautiful volume forms an instructive collection of striking facts."—*Spectator.*

"The Progress of Creation is a delightful volume. It abounds with instruction and breathes the spirit of fervent devotion."— *Observer.*

Works by the same Author.

CONCHOLOGIST'S COMPANION.

" To all lovers of shells, and students in the science of Conchology, this little volume, from the judicious and elegant pen of the author of the 'Wonders of the Vegetable Kingdom,' is an acceptable acquisition. Its flowing style and excellent sentiments render it an useful addition to our class books.—*Dublin Morning Star.*

" We strongly recommend this work to our readers."—*Monthly Critical Gazette.*

" This highly interesting and elegant little volume, displays in pleasing colours, the rich materials afforded by the science of shells for reflection and amusement."—*Monthly Review.*

" The work contains well-wrought descriptions of scenery, popular anecdotes of shells, their uses, appearance, and geographical distribution, interspersed with occasional poetry, original or selected; amongst the former of which are some displaying a correct taste and no little power."—*Athanæum.*

ANNALS OF MY VILLAGE,

A CALENDAR OF NATURE FOR EVERY MONTH IN THE YEAR.

" It is a singular gratification to meet a lover of nature so sincere and devoted as the intelligent author of this volume. Having lived so much amidst scenes of natural beauty and rural verdure, her language, her imagery, and even her definitions, partake of the rich associations of her fertile mind. The volume will prove an acceptable gift to the young of both sexes; but to the structure of the female mind it is pre-eminently adapted."—*Evangelical Magazine.*

" If some writers overlook the Great Author of nature in their works, others show how the being, wisdom, and goodness of the Most High, are displayed in the works of creation, such as Ray, Derham, and Paley. Among these will deservedly rank the author of the work now before us, a work which to every admirer of rural scenery must be no less fascinating than instructive."